RANCHO SANTA MARGARITA REMEMBERED

Rancho
Santa Margarita
Remembered

AN ORAL HISTORY

Jerome W. Baumgartner

FITHIAN PRESS · SANTA BARBARA, CALIFORNIA · 1989

To the kind and gentle people of the Santa Margarita.

Design and typography by
Jim Cook/Book Design & Typography, Santa Barbara, California

Published by Fithian Press
A division of Daniel & Daniel, Publishers, Inc.
Post Office Box 1525
Santa Barbara, CA 93102

LIBRARY OF CONGRESS CATALOGIGN-IN-PUBLICATION DATA
Baumgartner, Jerome O'Neill, date
    Rancho Santa Margarita remembered : an oral history / [edited by] Jerome W.
Baumgartner.
        p. cm.
    Reminiscences of the editor's father.
    Includes bibliographical references.
    ISBN 1-56474-182-6 (pbk. : alk. paper)
    1. Santa Margarita River Region (Calif.)—Social life and custons. 2. Rancho Santa
Margarita (Calif.) 3. Ranch life—California—Santa Margarita River Region.
4. Baumgartner, Jerome O'Neill, date—Family. 5. Baumgartner family.
I. Baumgartner, Jerome W., date. II. Title.
F868.S34B384 1996
972'.2—dc20   96-7749
                                                          CIP

ACKNOWLEDGMENTS

This book was shaped from a series of interviews with people who lived on Rancho Santa Margarita in its last days. The clear recollections of Carl Romer, Inez Grant and Harry Whitman provided the book with insights and view-points that give it depth and color. I am especially grateful to my father, Jerome O. Baumgartner, whose vivid memories of his early childhood are the essence of this book and whose story-telling abilities long ago painted the images inspiring this work.

And to my cousin, Tony Moiso, who pointed me in the right direction with the words, "Somebody should get all this down before it's too late," and for his moral and financial support in bringing the book to fruition.

And to Bill Downey, whose advice and instruction were so vital to the book's final form.

Contents

FOREWORD

My FATHER WAS RAISED at a time and in a place that he thought was so special that he has talked about it all his life. I was raised listening to those stories and hearing his history. In 1974, my wife and I invited my father to our home in Santa Barbara to record on tape what I had heard throughout my life. He reminisced for an entire weekend. The experience was such a success that we interviewed him several times more.

I had always thought these remembrances were interesting, but, when I began transcribing the tapes, I also found them very enjoyable reading. So, I began to organize them into an oral history of the ranch on which he was raised. It was a great ranch in Southern California—a quarter million acre ranch with tens of thousands of cattle and hundreds of horses. But the history was only part of the story he was telling. This ranch and its place in California history is the unmistakable focus of the story. But in many ways, it is only the setting for a childhood of vaqueros, Chinese cooks, aunts, uncles and other kind people who made such deep impressions on a young boy. People are great in small ways and it takes someone special to see the little greatnesses and remember them. These cooks, vaqueros and relatives were such people and my father has that special talent of remembering. And, as I read about these people in the transcripts, I began to see these characters as important to the feeling of the period as the ranch setting. So, this is not just a history of a Southern

California cattle ranch; it is a child's view of a period in the history of rural America.

This is a book of memories, not a book of history. History is an attempt at an objective view of time and place. These are memories and, as such, are necessarily subjective, adding what most histories lack: a sense of what it was like to live at another time and what it meant. All the words spoken in the book were either spoken by my father, Jerome O. Baumgartner; or by Carl Romer, an employee on Rancho Santa Margarita when my father was young; Inez Grant, a niece of Jane Magee, who spent many a summer's day at the Las Flores part of the ranch visiting her aunt and playing with the other children, including my father; or Harry Whitman, the manager of the Santa Margarita after Jerome O'Neill died.

RANCHO SANTA MARGARITA

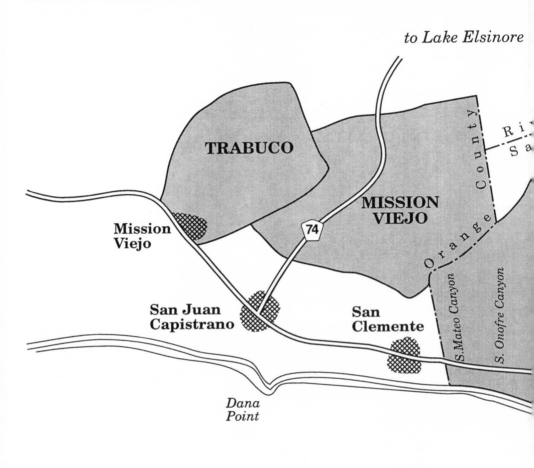

to Lake Elsinore

TRABUCO

**MISSION
VIEJO**

**Mission
Viejo**

74

Orange County

Ri
Sa

S. Mateo Canyon

S. Onofre Canyon

**San Juan
Capistrano**

**San
Clemente**

*Dana
Point*

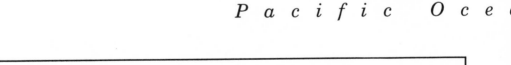

P a c i f i c   O c e a

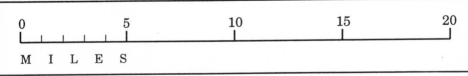

| 0 | 5 | 10 | 15 | 20 |

M I L E S

RANCHO SANTA MARGARITA REMEMBERED

CHAPTER ONE

An Autumn Friday, 1974

H E WAS OLD NOW. The suitcase felt heavy and he wondered what he had packed to make it so tiring to carry and why had he taken so much for such a short trip. But then there were some gifts and books for his son and daughter-in-law. The conductor opened the vestibule door as the train chattered and squealed to a stop. The old man stepped down right behind the conductor. He didn't really expect his son to meet him, because, after all, it was late afternoon and both Jome and his wife had jobs. He could walk around the station and watch people: college girls leaving boyfriends for dutiful weekend visits to their parents, arriving families with children on fall visits to the Santa Barbara beaches.

In spite of himself, he looked up hopefully and saw that they had come for him. Jome was wearing the grey Irish cloth cap that he had bought in Ireland the summer before. Sydney was there in a peach colored skirt and blouse. And they had brought their dog, O'Banion, on his leash. The whole household had come—as if he were a visiting dignitary. More than he could hope for, he thought, and broke into a smile. There was the awkward moment when father and son greeted each other with smiles and warmth and a handshake. The handshake was their custom but always an insufficient expression of the affection both of them felt. Sydney kissed his

1

cheek and O'Banion jumped up to be petted, wagging his tail as if welcoming his master. The old man greeted the dog by holding its head in both hands and speaking to it in that baby talk he always used to address dogs and small children. O'Banion stood very still, looking up at the old man bent over him, his face only inches from the dog's nose. The words and hands around his ears conveyed the affection that the father-son handshake had not. O'Banion felt the love of the old man completely and was satisfied.

On the way home in the car, the conversation was of the train trip and conversations with the other passengers. His talk was humorous, interesting and beneficial in renewing his closeness with his son. Both were grateful for the opportunity to overcome the awkwardness that a close relationship develops after a long separation. "Oh, it hasn't been so long since I've seen him," the father thought, 'two months.' But it seemed much longer.

By the time they reached the house, they had all found a lot to say, stumbling over each other with news and stories of their lives since his last visit. And when he had settled into his room, the old man opened his bag and removed the gifts. He went shyly to the living room, not wanting to interrupt their conversation or their lives but wishing, too, that he could be with them. He moved into the kitchen, hoping the gifts would make up for the inconvenience of his visit. They were part of the reason he had come. There was a photograph of himself as a very young child sitting with his grandfather on the wooden steps by the carriage shed and another of the family home on 17th Street in San Francisco.

To Jome, this was not just another weekend visit with his father. In the past, his father had talked for hours about his boyhood. The stories he told were warmly personal memories. They were not only the father's memories, but had become part of Jome's childhood through numerous retellings. They were like bedtime stories but much more vivid and exciting—not simply concoctions to tease a child's imagination, but tales of real people and events. And his father was always careful to use the right words to paint the pictures in his son's mind. Jome didn't want to lose the

2

*words and his father had agreed to come down expressly to say them again
for his son and daughter-in-law and in front of a tape recorder.*

*"Dad, how about a drink?" and Jome went to the kitchen to make his
father's customary bourbon and water. He made one for Sydney, too, and
poured himself a beer. His dad sat by the fireplace and he put the drink
down on the sidetable next to his father's favorite wicker rocker. Jome
struck a match on the hearth to light the fire he had laid earlier. Then
sitting across from the old man at the other side of the fireplace, Jome said,
"Dad, Syd and I would like to hear you tell again all about the ranch so that
we can get it on tape. I know most of the stories but I get some of them
confused and I don't remember all of them."*

*The old man nodded his head in agreement, saying: "I was thinking
about that coming down on the train and it might be a good idea to record
some of this, if you're willing to do it. There are not many people alive now
who lived on the ranch when I was a kid. Most of them are dead, and
unless someone gets this down permanently, then it's going to be lost."
And with that he took a sip of his drink and began:*

This is a little history of the Santa Margarita Rancho—as life was lived
there when I was a child, and as life was lived very much the same on any
ranch of that time. We had no corner on ranch life. People who lived on
smaller ranches around us lived pretty much as we did. So, things that
happened on the Santa Margarita were probably happening in other
places all over the West and Middle West. We didn't claim to have
anything unusual. But it just so happened that my generation—I being
the youngest—we grew up on the ranch in the last of the horse and
buggy days. The great changes in the modern era started about 1911.
Before that time, things were done on the Santa Margarita pretty much
as they had been for a hundred years, maybe more. The first automobile
came on the ranch in 1911 and, by that time, I was eight or nine years old.
The ranch didn't get mechanized for some years after that. By the time
the late teens came along, you still rode horses for the cattle but gasoline-
powered farm machinery appeared and the horse and buggy days were

over for good. So, my generation got in on the last of those horse and buggy times.

He paused to think of what to say next and to light a cigarette—a Lucky Strike. My father has smoked Lucky Strikes for as long as I can remember, but only when he has a cocktail, which might be three or four times a week. Other than at cocktail time, he rarely smokes. He puffed on his cigarette, squinting through the cloud of smoke around his face and went on:

4

As a matter of fact, when you get to be my age, you look back at your childhood and find that a lot of it's distorted. You can't remember clearly. You think you do but you have to give yourself a lot of leeway. I know the basic facts, but some of these things probably didn't happen as often as I thought and a lot of things happened that I didn't see right in front of my eyes. People told me about them later but I remember them as if I had actually seen them myself. We were not particularly sheltered as children, but kids weren't supposed to know about some things and I guess we really didn't. There were troubles that we weren't concerned with. The family didn't drag us into them. Maybe the family wasn't quite as happy as I thought they were, because I was happy. So, this history may seem happier than it really was and maybe some of my recollections are a little distorted, but this is the Santa Margarita Rancho as I saw it as a child.

There seems to be a question about the size of the ranch. Every time I read something, it's a different figure. The size varied from time to time because the ranch would acquire some pieces and sell others. But it was between 200,000 and 270,000 acres. They used to say that it was about 355 square miles, a quarter the size of Rhode Island. You could stand in the center of the ranch and look in all directions and everything you saw was part of the ranch. It ran from the San Luis Rey Valley just north of Oceanside to El Toro, which is about 35 miles. And it was 15 miles wide from the coast, but the inland boundary was staggered, not a straight line at all. And the coastline on its western border was 20 miles from San Luis Rey Valley to what we called the San Mateo Valley—in other words, to the San Diego-Orange County line.

The original name of the ranch was "Santa Margarita y Las Flores," Saint Margaret and the Flowers. That's one of the earliest place names in California. It was recorded by the Portola expedition in 1769. The original land grant was all in San Diego County and the northern boundary of the original ranch was the county line between Orange County and San Diego County. During the Mexican times, the Picos owned the Santa Margarita y Las Flores and they acquired the Mission Viejo Ranch and then a third piece called the Trabuco, which was north

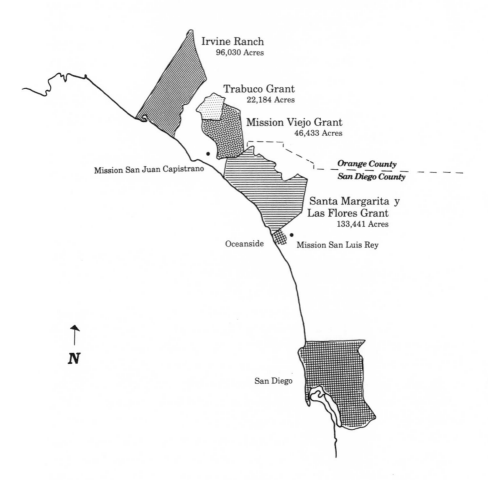

**Rancho Santa Margarita y las Flores
202,058 Acres**

Irvine Ranch
96,030 Acres

Trabuco Grant
22,184 Acres

Mission Viejo Grant
46,433 Acres

Mission San Juan Capistrano

Orange County
San Diego County

Santa Margarita y
Las Flores Grant
133,441 Acres

Oceanside

Mission San Luis Rey

N

San Diego

of the Mission Viejo, adjacent to El Toro. The Santa Margarita and the
Mission Viejo and the Trabuco were all part of one big ranch when my
grandfather O'Neill bought it and it all became known as simply the
Santa Margarita Ranch.

The ranch owned that twenty-mile stretch of beach from Oceanside to San Clemente. The ranch boundary jogged inland as it crossed the county line at what is now the town of San Clemente. Now, the Marines have taken the entire San Diego County part of the ranch and made it Camp Pendleton and the only part of the ranch that's still in private hands is the Mission Viejo and the Trabuco. Your cousins have that and they call it "Rancho Mission Viejo" but they really don't own any of the original Santa Margarita grant.

That's the physical part of the ranch, the land and where it was. But the ranch was much more than land to me. The people who lived on the ranch made such deep impressions on me that they, too, were the ranch. There was Sing, our Chinese cook, and my grandfather and Uncle Jerome and Uncle Jerome's younger brother, Dick. Strange as it may seem, my parents didn't seem a part of the ranch. My father's name was Baumgartner, of course, and he had married one of the O'Neill girls, and it was the O'Neills who owned the Santa Margarita. Most of the time I lived on the ranch, my parents lived up in San Francisco and we children saw them only at Christmas and other special occasions. We were raised by the women who lived on the ranch: my mother's oldest sister, Alice and Aunt Jane Magee and Auntie Wee Magee. All these people are as much a part of my memory of my early childhood as the ranch itself.

CHAPTER TWO

Some Important People to Me

SING WAS USUALLY up in his room in the early afternoon. He'd finished cooking lunch for the family and all the workers on the ranch and didn't have to begin dinner until four o'clock. When he had a few hours off, my brother John and I would sneak up to his room. We would creep up the plank stairs to what we called 'the Chinamen's room.' On top of all his other duties, Sing was a nursemaid for me and my brothers. Whenever he had time off, we'd be there. Sing was our favorite man on the ranch. He was a friend, but an adult, too, so he was a special friend. Chinamen of that era loved kids and, I gather, in China, the old China-men spoiled children, particularly the boys. At least, Sing spoiled us.

Sing had a helper, a sculleryman named Hom, whose primary duty was to wash the dishes and pots and pans, and he lived up in that room with Sing. In the afternoons Hom would be down in the kitchen washing up the lunch dishes. The Chinamen's room was originally built to store vegetables like potatoes and onions. The outside walls of the room were made of lattice, so, during the day, the room was dappled in sunlight, making checkered patterns on the floor. They still stored vegetables up there but the Chinamen had their bunks there too, and a little table and chair and a lantern and that was about all the furnishings they had.

8

When we got to the top of the stairs, we would knock on Sing's door and, without getting up from the table, he would tell us to come in. He knew who it was. John would open the door. He was two years older—this was in 1908—so I was only five and still having trouble with doorknobs. Sing would be at the table writing a letter to his wife in China, his apron hanging from a nail on the wall. He'd never interrupt his writing because of us and we were used to that. I think that when Sing wrote home, it was his time to be alone with his wife and I don't know if we understood it then but we would just play quietly until he was finished. He had an abacus for doing his figures and we liked to play with all of its beads. Once he tried to teach us to use it but I never got the hang of it. I think John did, but while we waited for Sing to finish John would do nothing more serious than play with it.

It was fascinating to see Sing write. He had a tablet of white paper with faint red lines and he wrote intricate characters with a little brush. The characters were ornate as little Victorian houses and his brush moved quickly and surely, stopping only for more ink.

He would sit on his bunk while he wrote, his pillow right next to him. It was a Chinese pillow—a little box covered with leather. It wasn't soft like a regular pillow but it had a little give to it. When he slept, he'd put this box under his neck, so that his neck and the lower part of his head were resting on it and he'd snooze like that. I tried the pillow once but it felt pretty uncomfortable to me.

When he was finished writing, Sing would lay down his brush, put the top on the ink bottle and roll a cigarette. This was in the days before ready-made cigarettes and everybody rolled their own. Most of the vaqueros smoked Bull Durham, but Sing smoked Union Leader Tobacco. It was pipe tobacco that came in a red can about as big as a coffee can. He kept his writing brushes in an empty Union Leader can at the corner of his table. Bull Durham came with two kinds of cigarette papers: wheat papers and rice papers. You could buy these papers separately from the tobacco, but Sing didn't use either one. He would tear a piece of writing paper off a sheet of his tablet and put some tobacco on it. Then he rolled it up into a cone. He'd put the small end of the cone in his mouth and light the other end with a wooden kitchen match. And he always lit the match with one hand, scratching the tip with his thumb nail. He did it without thinking and with such nonchalance that it was magic to us. The cigarette wasn't very long and Sing would take only three or four puffs and put it out. After he had finished writing, Sing would tell us about his wife and sons back in China and he'd have a smoke. He would talk and we'd listen, but meanwhile, we'd watch this marvelous show of rolling the cigarette, lighting the match with one hand and puffing on this stubby, little cigarette. And, when he told us about his family, he never looked at us. He'd watch what he was doing while he rolled his smoke, but, after it was lit, he'd keep talking and gaze off into the distance as if he were talking to himself.

He spoke English very well. If you had heard him but couldn't see him, you'd know he was Chinese all right. He had an accent that made his English a little pidgin, but we always understood everything he said to us. I suppose he didn't speak English at all when he first came to the Santa Margarita, but he'd been on the ranch thirty years by that time. Sing would work at the ranch house for four or five years without a day off and then he'd take six months off to go visit his family in China. His wife and one of his sons had been killed in the Boxer Rebellion, but, on his next visit, Sing remarried and, by 1908, he had other children. So, Sing had a pretty rough and lonely life, but he was always very kind to us kids.

God, he worked hard! At mealtimes, Sing had two separate menus: one for the family—between six and twelve people—and a different menu for the men's diningroom. Sometimes there would be fifty or sixty people to feed and Sing cooked two different menus for them, three times a day for four or five years, without a day off! During that time, he never left the ranch house and he made it one of his duties to see after us kids as well. Then he'd go to China to see his wife and family.

There were other people on the ranch who took care of us but they were primarily ranchers and so very busy people. When I was young, my grandfather, Richard O'Neill, was still running the ranch. He was my grandfather on my mother's side and he was a very old man when I was on the ranch. He was not tall; actually he was more on the short side. But he was referred to as "Big Dick" by his peers, I suppose because he was a big rancher, not a big man. And he had a beard, not a full beard, but a Vandyke. He was of that generation that wore beards and his was always well trimmed and gave him a distinguished look. In the last years of his life, his oldest son, my Uncle Jerome, had gradually taken over the managing of the Santa Margarita. The two of them discussed the decisions that had to be made, but by that time, it was Uncle Jerome who did the actual managing. And in the last two or three years of his life, my grandfather had practically ceased to have anything to do with the running of the ranch.

My grandfather's room was down the hall and I'd hear him coming along the hallway in his boots. In his day, ranching people always wore boots. He never had a pair of shoes in his life. But they weren't cowboy boots. They had a low heel and round toes and came up just above his ankles. They weren't for riding horses, just for walking, and I would hear him coming down the hall and follow him to his room. He was in his eighties and he would walk very slowly and shuffle his feet. In his bedroom was a bootjack, a piece of board slanted up with a V in it and I'd watch him take his boots off. I liked to play on his bootjack, pretending it was a sleigh or a wagon.

The memory of this brought a gentle smile to his whole face but, as he snuffed his cigarette out, the smile vanished as he realized how childish that recollection might seem to us.

After your great-grandfather died, Uncle Jerome, his eldest son, became the new owner and manager of the ranch. In Victorian families, business arrangements were not discussed. So, it was never made clear to me how Uncle Jerome came to be the big boss of the outfit rather than one of the other three children. There was my mother, Mary, and my Uncle Dick, and Aunt Alice, who was the oldest of all the children. But, as I understand it, my grandfather believed in the English system of primogeniture, in which the eldest son inherits everything and is responsible for seeing that the other children are cared for. And, of course, Uncle Jerome had learned ranching at my grandfather's side while he was growing up, so, from the ranching standpoint, he was the logical choice to succeed his father.

Uncle Jerome was a very serious man. He devoted his whole life to running that ranch and he made it his business to be aware of every detail. He'd delegate his authority, but then he'd check on the man to whom he had delegated it. And he was a straight-talking man. He wanted an honest answer, and if he didn't get it he'd know. You were always on trial with him. I wouldn't say that everybody was scared to death of him, but, if they weren't, they respected him to the point that they weren't going to be caught in a position that could arouse his disapproval. He was a very subdued man and he didn't often get mad. He spoke very quietly and calmly but once in a while he would get angry and then he could really bark. Not very often, but often enough so that everyone would remember and always act to avoid his wrath.

Every day on the ranch Uncle Jerome wore a business suit with a vest, a white shirt and a necktie. That was the uniform for the big boss. No matter what he was doing, Uncle Jerome wore a suit and tie. He was a short, husky man with big bones in his hands and face. He was as strong as a bull, but he was lame. He had infantile paralysis, so he had a deformed foot and I think he'd had it all his life. He wore a brace and could walk, but he threw his leg out to the side. He couldn't walk a mile or anything like that, but he was pretty agile, considering. Even though he was a very strong man, he had difficulty climbing up on a horse. He could probably have mounted by himself but it would have been an awkward struggle and not in keeping with the dignified figure he wished to present. So, at the ranch house, they kept a wooden box with steps near the corral so that he could mount a horse more easily. Out in the vaquero camps, he would use the running board of a car. His lame leg did not affect his horseback riding though. He was a very good horseman. But I think that leg influenced his personality and his attitude toward life. When he was a young boy, his leg set him apart from the other boys and he couldn't play the games the other boys played. My sister Bessie was the oldest of the Baumgartner children and, as such, knew things about Uncle Jerome the rest of us were too young to realize. Bessie says that Uncle Jerome did have a serious courtship with a girl at one stage in his life. But she eventually turned him away and he blamed his failure on his leg. When my grandfather was the big boss, he was rough and ready, so Uncle Jerome always had to be tough, too. When he was twenty, he came to the Santa Margarita with his father and he'd already had a very good background in the cattle business. He became very much my grandfather's aide and was clearly the heir apparent to the ranch. So he had a lot of responsibility and took life very seriously. He didn't drink at all and was never known for his sense of humor. He had this handicap to overcome and the responsibility of running this big ranch, at first as his father's right-hand man and, after his father died, as the big boss himself. Not having any other outlets for his activities because of his leg, he probably concentrated on his responsibilities more than most people would have.

Dad paused here and looked over at his glass of bourbon as if suddenly remembering it was there. He picked it up and his hand trembled slightly, making the ice tinkle. It was an old man's tremble which he had developed in recent years. Syd took this opportunity to excuse herself and went into the kitchen to prepare dinner.

When my grandfather died in 1910, rather than dividing the ranch lands between all his children, he willed the whole ranch to Uncle Jerome and he paid Uncle Dick and my mother so much a year over many years for their interest in the ranch. It was all very Victorian, all very hush-hush. Nobody ever discussed family matters; everyone whispered about things like that. In those days people thought that it was nobody's business how much money you had—which it wasn't, of course—but they took it to ridiculous extremes, to the point that it was almost dangerous. Nobody really knew what was going on financially. So my Uncle Dick, Uncle Jerome's younger brother, got his money every year and never had any responsibilities on the ranch. When his father was alive, Uncle Jerome was the son who helped his father run the ranch and Uncle Dick was pretty much excluded. My grandfather used to say 'Every family should have a gentleman, and in this family it might as well be Dick.' So, Uncle Dick had no particular duties on the ranch and he had more of his share of free time in which to have fun.

For a while, Uncle Dick lived up in San Francisco and worked as a clerk in James Flood's bank. I think Uncle Jerome got him that job to give him something productive to do. Uncle Dick was not a rancher. He liked the night life of the big city. He'd work at the bank during the day and then go out carousing with his friends at night. Gentleman Jim Corbett, who was later to be the heavyweight champion of the world, was a good friend of Dick's and they'd go out together and raise hell. On Wednesday nights, Corbett liked to frequent the neighborhood firehouse and on Friday nights, the local blacksmith shop. The toughest young men of the neighborhood used to meet in those places and Corbett would always get into a fight. After licking all the regulars in the neighborhood, Corbett moved over to the lowest dives on the Barbary Coast where the roughest of San Francisco's underworld congregated. I don't think Uncle Dick was much of a fighter but he liked to run with the fastest and roughest crowd in town.

Reports of Uncle Dick's goings-on made their way down to the ranch. Uncle Jerome tried to save the family's reputation by recalling Dick home to the ranch where he did virtually nothing during the week but wait for the weekends when he could escape for the good times of San Diego and Los Angeles. I don't mean that he never worked around the ranch, but it wasn't often. He was a fancy dresser and didn't have any real work clothes. When he stayed on the ranch, he put on a pair of gloves first thing in the morning. I don't know if they were supposed to keep his hands from blistering or if he wore them because he thought they looked colorful.

14

Billy Magee lived over at the Las Flores and was employed by Uncle Jerome to manage part of the ranch. He and Uncle Dick were close companions. Billy didn't have much money except what Uncle Jerome paid him. So I think Dick provided the free drinks and Billy provided the hilarity and they would sneak off and have fun. Of course, Uncle Jerome didn't approve of any of this, so they tried to keep it quiet, but news of some of their wilder escapades always found its way back to the ranch house.

Aunt Alice was my mother's only sister. She was the oldest of the O'Neill children—four years older than Uncle Jerome. She was living on the ranch when I arrived in 1904 and she was there for many years afterward. My grandmother was quite old by the time I was born and she was brought down to the ranch from San Francisco where Aunt Alice could take care of her. Later on, when my grandfather also got to the point where he needed care, Auntie Wee came over from the Magee family at the Las Flores to help. But, from the time I was three months old, Aunt Alice not only looked after her parents, she also took care of me all the time I lived on the Santa Margarita. So she was practically my mother. She was married to a man named McDade who was a sheriff up in San Francisco. Apparently they weren't happily married because they didn't live together. Today you'd say they were separated, but in those days people just didn't talk about it. Once in a while, John McDade would come down to visit, but even then, he wasn't anybody's favorite person on the ranch. So, Aunt Alice had an unusual situation: she was married to this McDade but she was all alone and she had no children of her own, but she was raising her sister's children. And all this went on happily until just after my grandfather died in 1910. Then a family battle erupted that I'll tell you about later.

The Magee women were constantly in our family picture even though they were not related to us in any way. The Magees had become good friends of my grandfather when he bought the Santa Margarita. Jane Magee leased the Las Flores Mesa lands from the ranch and she raised beans there. She was a thin, nervous woman, but very handsome. She had lots of brothers and sisters and all the Magees were considered part of our family. So the children in our family called the Magees "Aunt This" and "Uncle That" and every so often we would go over to the Las Flores and stay with Aunt Jane for weeks at a time. Aunt Jane had a half sister named Luisa whom we called "Auntie Wee" and she was the Magee who moved over to the Santa Margarita ranch house to care for my grandparents in their last days. She acted as a nursemaid for us kids as well.

Syd came out of the kitchen and stood by my chair and patiently waited for a pause in my father's story.

Those were the main characters affecting my life as a child at the Santa Margarita. There were others: Steve Peters, old Tiano, and Billy and Louie Magee. But I'll tell you about them as they come into the story.

"Dinner's ready," Syd said.
Her interruption was well received because Dad and I were hungry. Both of us had been completely absorbed in the storytelling and had forgotten our stomachs. The call to dinner brought us immediately to our feet and to the dinner table. There was little talk at dinner—a few compliments on the food, a comment by my father about the flowers on the table. After dinner, we adjourned to the living room and took our seats as before, and my father resumed his story.

CHAPTER THREE

The Ranch House

*F*ROM TIME TO TIME *as I was growing up, my father would tell me stories of his early life on the Santa Margarita. But as he grew older, his childhood on the ranch seemed to be in his thoughts more and more and he talked about the ranch frequently. Over the past ten years or so, he had arranged several trips down to the old ranch, particularly to visit the house where he was raised. The Marines had taken most of the ranch during the Second World War, and ever since it has been used as Camp Pendleton Marine Corps Base. There was a different commanding general living at the ranch house on each of our visits, but all generously opened their home to us. They were very gracious and seemed genuinely interested in all my father recollected about the house.*

17

The Santa Margarita ranch house is now the home of the commanding general of Camp Pendleton, but in my day it was our family home and the headquarters of the ranch. The ranch house was built in the Spanish style in the shape of a square around a central patio. All the rooms opened onto the patio, and a covered walkway ran along the inside of the square. There were few interior doors in the house. That was typical of adobe buildings because interior doorways weakened the adobe walls, so most of the rooms opened onto the patio. To go from one room to another, we had to walk out onto the patio and over to the door of the next room. In one corner of the patio there was a bougainvillea vine which was big for as long as I can remember. They used to say that the bougainvillea was as old as the house, which would make it one of the oldest in California. The last time we visited the ranch house, it was still there. The Marines have taken good care of it. When visitors came to the ranch house during the day, they were always entertained on the patio. You could enter the patio through what we called 'the big gate' without going through the house. The big gate wasn't a gate at all, but wide double doors in the northwest courtyard wall, opening onto the covered walkway around the patio. When we went to the outhouse, we'd go out the big gate. Every day firewood and other ranch house supplies would be brought in through the big gate. So, actually, it was used far more often than the front door. The front door was at the end of a long hallway facing southwest. It wasn't anything very special, just a wooden door painted white. But, on either side of it were panes of colored glass from floor to ceiling. Each pane was twelve inches square and each a different color. They were primary colors like yellow and green and made the hallway bright and cheery. Looking down that hallway was like peering into a kaleidoscope.

Just inside the big gate was the olla. It was a simple wooden box about three feet square, full of river sand, with the big pottery olla jar set down into the sand. It was a primitive water cooler because the sand kept the water in the jar cool. There was a dipper hanging from a rawhide cord on the wall and everyone who wanted a drink of water used the same dipper. Sanitation was not considered much on the ranch and I often wonder why we didn't get sick more often than we did. In fact, we didn't seem to get sick as often as people do now.

We did have some running water, but not in the rooms. There was a water tank near the ranch house fed by windmills and there was enough water pressure to supply a few faucets. There were faucets on the outside of the house to water the garden and there was a faucet right beside the kitchen door with a half barrel below. The water dripped out of this faucet into the barrel so there was always water for the dogs. There was running water in the kitchen for cooking and washing dishes and the kitchen had the only hot water in the house. Also in the kitchen was a great big cooking range. When you're young everything looks bigger than it really is, but this range really was big. On the back of the wood-burning range there was a copper tank full of water and the range was stoked all day so that there was a constant supply of hot water. There was a dipper hooked over the side of the stove and if you needed hot water, you'd dip some from the tank. If you wanted a hot shave in your room, you'd walk down to the kitchen with your pitcher and dip yourself some hot water and take it back to your room.

The walls of the ranch house were all adobe like most of the structures built during the early years. There were no other materials with which to build. There were no trees for timber and there was no supply of stone or rock. But there was plenty of adobe clay everywhere, so the padres built everything with adobe brick. But, to make the walls strong enough to support the heavy tile roofs, the walls had to be very thick, sometimes six or eight feet thick. They were terrific insulation. In the wintertime, the walls and tile roofs would hold in the heat from the fireplaces and in the summer they kept the interior cool. The summertime temperatures would get up to 85 or 90, maybe 95 degrees on a very hot day. Not as hot as summer days in the San Joaquin Valley, but it got pretty damned hot. But it was always cool in the ranch house.

Across the top of the walls were great beams, twelve by twelve and maybe bigger than that. I don't know where they got timbers of that size, certainly not on the ranch or anywhere around there. They must have been big pines from the San Jacinto Mountains. These beams were up there for years and they didn't rot out. The beams that were there when I was a kid were probably the original ones that dated back to mission days. The big beams and the smaller ones supporting the tiles were tied together with leather thongs. At the time the ranch house was built, they didn't have nails, so the beams had to be lashed together with rawhide straps. The straps would shrink and stretch depending on the weather and the roof would groan and crack at night and scare the hell out of us kids. I slept in a room we called the dungeon because it didn't have any windows. In the ceiling of this room there was a little vent about six inches square. All the rooms had these vents in the ceilings so that air could circulate through the attic. They used to tell us kids that there was the ghost of an old lady with long grey hair that lived up in the attic, and at night she would walk around and look down through these vents while you were sleeping. I remember just drifting off to sleep when the groaning of these leather straps would jerk me awake. And then I would lie in the bed pretending to be asleep, but I'd have one eye open just enough so that I could see through a narrow slit in my eyelids and I'd look at that little vent hole to see if the old lady was coming to get me.

"Dad, would you like a nightcap?" I asked. Both my father and Syd said yes, so I went into the kitchen to make the after-dinner drinks. As I struggled to get the ice out of the icetrays, I heard Syd telling my dad about her new job. My father was relieved to have someone else talk for a while. I took the drinks into the livingroom and Syd quickly said, "You were telling us about the ranch house, Mr. B. Please go on."

Well, you've been to the ranch house so you don't have to be told exactly what it was like. It hasn't changed too much from the way it was in my childhood. The Marines have done a wonderful job maintaining it and keeping it essentially as it was when I lived there. Of course, they've changed some of the rooms because it is now the general's home. Many of the rooms no longer serve the same functions as they did when it was the ranch headquarters. But everything is about the same except that now there is plumbing and electricity. In my early youth, we used kerosene lamps rather than electric lights and we had an outhouse instead of indoor plumbing. The outhouse at the ranch was not a wooden building. It was adobe to match the ranch house. An old-fashioned privy was just a hole in the ground with a small building around it for protection. Privies were moved every so often because they needed to start a new hole. But the adobe outhouse they had at the ranch was very old when I was born and as far as I know they never moved it. It was probably unhealthy as hell, but nobody seemed to think anything about it. At that time, ranches were operating just as they had for a hundred years and that was particularly true of the Santa Margarita. My grandfather was not what you'd call progressive and he kept everything as it had always been, including the outhouse.

As far as privies are concerned, I'm afraid that some of the finer distinctions would be lost on the younger generation. Our privy was a three-holer instead of just a one-holer. There was a large hole for the men, a smaller one for the ladies and a little one for the small kids. And not only that, but they were in steps, one next to the other so that the men's was the tallest and the children's the shortest, with the women's in between. We didn't go in there at night. In every bedroom there was a chamber pot and if you had to use the toilet at night, you didn't stumble out to the outhouse. You used a chamber pot. There was a commode in each room. That was a piece of furniture like a small bureau with doors on the front and that's where you put the chamber pot after you used it. On top of the commode there was always a pitcher of water and a wash bowl and a towel that served the same purpose as a sink today. When I was very young, I was trained on the chamber pot, but when I was old enough, they'd put me in the outhouse and leave me in there with the instructions: 'Don't go near those other two holes.' So, I'd sit there and look at those other holes, scared to death. Nobody wanted to fall in. And, as you grew up, it gave you quite a sense of accomplishment to move up to the next higher seat.

The ranch house was situated on top of a little knoll. You'd hardly notice it but it was on the high ground. The ranch was part of the lands of Mission San Luis Rey and the first mention of the ranch house was in the mission records of 1827. So, it was built sometime before that year but exactly when hasn't been determined. The ranch house was not built all at one time. It probably began as a one-room adobe used by the vaqueros and shepherds who worked for the mission when they had to stay out tending livestock. When the Picos took over the ranch in the 1840s, they added to the house and it became more of a residence than a bunkhouse. But whoever originally selected the site on top of that rise picked a spot that kept the ranch house from being flooded by the Santa Margarita River. Back when the first rooms were built, I imagine that the nearness of the river was important for a convenient water supply. Like many rivers in Southern California, the Santa Margarita wasn't much of a river in most years, but it always had water in it. The water wouldn't be more than half a foot deep in late August but there was always water. But every so often we would have tremendous winter rains and the river would spill over its banks and flood the lowland. They used to say these heavy rains came every seven years and I think they were right about that. Nineteen-sixteen was the year of the worst flood in anybody's memory. The valley was flooded from hill to hill but even in that year the water never came up to the ranch house. I was going to school up in San Francisco at the time, so I didn't see any of it but I heard all about it. The railroad tracks and telephone poles were all washed out and the water got up as far as the barn. For a while they were worried that the ranch house itself would flood and they even made preparations to evacuate. There was a wagon standing by to take my grandmother out if the water got too high. There were big oak trees floating by the house and pieces of railroad track with the ties still on, floating around like a horse's tail. It was about a year and a half before the railroad was rebuilt. In the meantime we had to send a wagon down to Oceanside every day for the supplies that would normally have come up on the train.

Between the ranch house and the barn was the vaqueros' bunkhouse. It was an adobe building covered by board and batten so that it looked like a wooden building from the outside. It had quite a few rooms. Most of the men lived in one large room, but the majordomo would have his own room and so would most of the artisans who worked on the ranch. There was always a full-time harnessmaker who lived in the bunkhouse. One of the rooms was a tackroom where the vaqueros kept all of their riding gear and where the harnessmaker could work. And the blacksmith and the carpenter would sleep in the bunkhouse, too. When the men had finished work for the day, the vaqueros would come up from the barn with their saddles and harness and the field workers would come in from the fields. They'd all be dusty. There was a long trough along the bunkhouse with running water from the water tank and they'd all wash up for dinner. Then they'd wipe their hands and faces on one of those roller towels. I don't think they have them any more because they're so unsanitary but nobody thought of those things back then. And so they'd wash up and come up to the ranch house for dinner.

There was an irrigation ditch that ran by the bunkhouse and the men's bathhouse was built over it. The water tank supplied water to the shower nozzles inside. The men could go in there and pull down the chain and take a shower—a cold shower. There was no hot running water for any-body on the ranch in those days. If the men wanted to take a dip, they could jump into the ditch. They didn't shower every day, because nobody did in those days, even the best of them didn't. But there were means there to keep fairly clean.

As you walk down from the main ranch house in the direction of the vaquero bunkhouse, to the right of it was the blacksmith shop. It was an old adobe and they used to say that it was the oldest building on the ranch. In the mission days it was used as a winery. My grandfather had the interior of the old winery divided into several rooms for storage and workshops and he added a lean-to against the exterior wall for the blacksmith shop. But we called the whole complex 'the blacksmith's shop.' It was like the bunkhouse in that it, too, had a facing of board and batten. I don't know why or when that was done, but I think it was to protect the adobe from the rain. That's probably why the building has been standing so long. There were rooms in the blacksmith shop used by all the artisans on the ranch. These were not laborers; they were skilled workers. Besides a blacksmith, there was always a carpenter and other skilled people who did specialized work. But the blacksmith was the king of the walk because he was the mechanic of the crew and was held in higher regard than the others. The blacksmith's shop is still there. The Marines have stripped off the board walls and made it into a lovely chapel.

In the evenings, the family would sit out on the front porch of the ranch house. Just after the sun set and before it got dark, you could look way down the Santa Margarita Valley and watch the valley and the oak trees and the hillsides change color as the light faded. In the 1880s, a Scotchman named John Clay was touring the West looking for good cattle land to buy for wealthy English investors and he visited the Santa Margarita. Later, he wrote a book about what he saw called *My Life On The Range*. In his book, he made a mistake. He said he could see the ocean from the front porch of the ranch house. We were eight miles from the ocean there and the valley twisted and turned, so you couldn't see more than two or three miles. But off in the distance the valley widened out and then there were two fingers of the hills that came from either side of the valley toward each other. The road and the railroad tracks ran between these fingers and right up the middle of the valley and these two straight lines off to the horizon made the valley seem very long.

The whole family would sit out on the porch on summer evenings talking in hushed tones the way people do when it's getting dark and I would be playing on the floor at the foot of my grandfather's rocker. I can remember hearing the birds all chattering the way they do just before dark. Aunt Jane used to tell us that they were all saying goodnight to each other. So, I remember listening to the birds saying goodnight and hearing the creak of Grandpa's rocker, and the adults all talking very softly like they didn't want to wake up the birds. My mother would have just come from San Francisco and my uncle would ask about all the people that they knew in the City and all the gossip. And when it got dark and cool, the ladies would put on their shawls. Some nights the vaqueros would play their guitars down in the bunkhouse and we could hear them singing. I remember they always played one song in particular. It must have been popular at the time. It had a beautiful melody. They called it *La Golondrina*. Later on it became famous when they added words and called it *The Loveliest Night Of The Year*. And this song would come drifting up from the bunkhouse.

He ran his hand down the back of his head, rocked slowly in the rocker and started to hum the melody of The Loveliest Night Of The Year.

But if you were sitting on the front porch you could always see anyone coming to the ranch house because you could see them two miles away on the road. Well, you couldn't actually see them, but their horses or, later, their car would throw up a cloud of dust that was easily seen from the porch. And it would be another half hour before they would arrive. Every so often we had to phone Dr. Nichols down in Oceanside because maybe one of my grandparents had an attack or one of the men injured himself and Dr. Nichols would drive out to the ranch at night—not very often but once in a while. After the automobile came in, Dr. Nichols had a Model T like everybody else. And the whole family would sit on the porch and wait for Dr. Nichols' Model T to come around that point way down the valley. I was a very small boy when my grandparents were having these attacks but I can remember being out on the porch with the adults and everybody waiting, not saying much at all. Because the adults were so somber and were allowing us kids to stay up late, I knew that this must be very serious. Nobody said much and if they did it was in a whisper. As a small child, I remember playing on the floor of the porch and being very quiet because all the adults were quiet and it reminded me of how everyone acted in church. It would take Dr. Nichols two hours from Oceanside but then his headlights would come around that point and everyone breathed a sigh of relief. This didn't happen too often, but when it did it made a great impression on me.

Dr. Nichols was only called for the very serious cases; all the day-to-day medical problems had to be handled right on the ranch. A doctor was never called when we children had the typical childhood illnesses. Those were taken very much in stride by the adults. And it seems to me that they had only three kinds of medicines that they'd keep in the medicine chest—home medicines that were used for almost every problem we ever had. There was witch hazel. They always kept a bottle of witch hazel on hand and I always liked the clean smell of it. They put it on itches and rashes and it was used as a disinfectant if we cut our fingers or got a splinter. Have you ever heard of Cascara? That was another remedy but I don't think it's used any more. It was for stomach ailments and was made out of some sort of root. The doctor would prescribe it and they always kept a bottle at the ranch. It was brown, like mud and the most vile stuff you ever tasted. It was like drinking ink. God, it was awful! And castor oil. If we felt bad we'd never admit it unless we thought we were dying because somebody would give us a dose of castor oil. I don't suppose they give it to people anymore and that's certainly a step forward for medical progress and a blessing for kids everywhere. I remember they'd coax us to drink it by squeezing lemon juice into a glass with some sugar, making a little strong lemonade. Then they'd add some castor oil, I don't know how much, but they'd say 'Now swallow this and you won't taste a thing.' But that was never true. Nothing could kill the taste of castor oil. I wonder if it did any good. Everyone thought that it did but I think they thought that only because it tasted so awful. I don't recall any other medicine that was commonly used. Not on us kids anyway. Witch hazel, cascara and castor oil were the Santa Margarita miracle drugs and, even if we didn't like them too much, they didn't seem to do any permanent harm.

There was a custom from the Spanish days when everyone was Catholic. Every cattle ranch had a cross on the top of the hill nearest the ranch house. And the Santa Margarita had one. If you walked from the ranch house, down past the vaquero bunkhouse and the barn and through the corrals, you came to a hill with a white cross on the top overlooking the ranch house. It was there for as long as I can remember and it may have been put up by the Picos or maybe even earlier than that. We used to climb that hill and sit beneath the cross. It wasn't anything fancy, just made of wood planks that had been whitewashed. But from the cross, there was a magnificent view of the ranch house and the valley. In the foreground were the corrals and the barn and a little farther, the bunkhouse, and farther yet the ranch house with the river curving and twisting its way on one side and a row of palm trees on the other. Off in the distance, the green alfalfa fields and, at the horizon, the Vallecito Mountains. My brother, John, and I would climb up there in the mornings and look back down on our little world and it was beautiful to see.

"Dad, can I freshen your drink?"

"Okay. That'll be fine, but I don't want to keep you up all night."

"We want to stay up as long as you feel like talking. Besides, tomorrow is Saturday and we can sleep as late as we want."

Syd said, "Mr. B., tell me about Sing."

CHAPTER FOUR

Sing Yung

*M*Y FATHER *had been talking for hours. He was reliving the most pleasant time of his life and he was enjoying himself. And I think it pleased him very much that we enjoyed reliving it with him. He was two different men. When we visited my mother and father at their home in Atherton, he said very little. My mother did nearly all the talking and he seemed to enjoy listening to her. Oh, I don't know how much he really listened to her. When she was going on at length about some subject that didn't particularly interest him, I'd look over at him and his head would be tilted back with a dreamy gaze in his eyes, and he would stroke the back of his head. He wasn't listening at all but was somewhere else entirely. I often wondered where he was, but he'd have a smile on his lips and a softness in his eyes and, wherever he was, it must have been very pleasant. But then he was another person when he visited us. He could talk for hours— interesting talk of his childhood on the ranch and of all the kind and wonderful people who were there then he was young.*

When Syd mentioned that she wanted him to tell about Sing, he paused very deliberately and reached for his drink. He took a slow sip and put the drink down. Then he sat back in the rocking chair and his left arm came up behind his head and he began stroking the hair at the back of his head.

He was staring off into the distance and letting Sing's memory fill his mind. And when he was ready, he started his story of Sing:

You'll want to hear about Sing. Sing was a continual story because he was the cook on the ranch for years. But the story of Sing was one very common to California ranches of that period. Chinese cooks on ranches were not unusual at all. Many people in the cities had Chinese cooks, too. Usually, Chinese men were cooks, not Chinese women. Sing came to the Santa Margarita from China before the Chinese Exclusion Act was passed in 1882. It prohibited all Chinese from entering this country. Sing had been here before the Exclusion Act and had papers allowing him to go back and forth to China. Aunt Jane used to tell me this story: Sing came to the Santa Margarita when he was just eighteen and he worked first at the Las Flores house. At that time, besides her bean crop, Aunt Jane had a small dairy at the Las Flores and she made butter and sent it to Oceanside to be sold. For a few years Sing worked in the dairy making butter and churning it by hand. I can't remember what year he came to the Santa Margarita to do the cooking, but he was there about forty years. So, he cooked for the Santa Margarita until he went back to China for the last time in 1919. He would go to China on a leave of absence every four or five years. The ranch would get another cook and off Sing would go to China for six months.

His full name was Sing Yung. In China, Sing was the family name and Yung was his given name, but he was called Sing on the Santa Margarita. Vaguely I remember Sing telling us about his family. He had a son by his first wife; he was always telling us about his son in China. His first wife was killed in the Boxer Rebellion, so he went back and married again and every four years he'd pack up and go to China to see his family. He was always trying to get his son into this country, but he was never able to do it because of the Exclusion Act.

Well, he'd sail for China on a ship from San Francisco, the only big city in California then. In those days when you were 'going to the City,' no matter where you were in California, whether you were in San Diego County or Los Angeles, you were going to San Francisco. San Francisco was much larger than Los Angeles in those days and it was the headquarters of the Chinese because of the large population of San Francisco's Chinatown. Los Angeles had a Chinatown too, but it was very small compared to the Chinatown in San Francisco and it still is. So the mecca of Chinamen, as far as Chinese in California were concerned, was San Francisco and the vicinity. When Sing went to China, he'd get out his store-bought clothes. He had an old suit that he had bought years ago—a suit like our suits of the day and a hat, like a regular hat. He'd get all dressed up to go to China, and the family would drive him to the train and he'd go up to San Francisco. He would stay in San Francisco a few days until his ship sailed to China, and he always had the most inexpensive accommodations. I guess he travelled in steerage. Sometimes, before his ship left, he'd take a side trip to Stockton. There were a lot of Chinese in Stockton, too, and he had friends there. While he was in San Francisco, he'd get in touch with my mother and say good-bye. It was a big day on the ranch for us kids when Sing came back, and he'd always bring presents for the whole family. The Chinese were great at gift-giving. He'd bring us boys dragon kites, and dolls for the girls, and fans and parasols for the women.

His frame of action for the four years between trips to China was literally the ranch house, the area right around it and, maybe, over to the Las Flores once in a while. He never went into Oceanside unless he was going to China, not even to the bank with his pay. Sing was a skilled workman, so I imagine he got about sixty dollars a month, which was pretty good pay in those days. He got more than a vaquero would. I'm not sure what he got, but he wasn't paid the thirty dollars a month of an unskilled laborer. He sent a lot of his money back to China to help his family because it didn't cost him a dime to live on the ranch. He wore loose pants, baggy Chinese pants, and a regular shirt, so his clothing bill wasn't five or ten dollars a year. He would send a great part of his salary back to China, but he saved some because he had to pay for his trip home every four years. But he didn't go to Oceanside to the bank himself. Somebody would go down to Oceanside to the bank for him, so he'd have money to buy a ticket for China when the time came.

Sing needed tremendous amounts of flour because he made all his own bread and pies. And maybe twenty sacks of flour would come up on the train from Oceanside every so often. The ranch wagon brought it up and it was kept in the storeroom. You know what a sack of flour looks like? It was always a white sack with a brand name stamped on it, Gold Medal or whatever, made out of cotton cloth. They still make the same kind of flour sacks. And Sing would open up a sack and make bread out of it, or pies, and very quickly there'd be a collection—a tremendous collection of these sacks. But you couldn't find an empty flour sack on the ranch, no matter how many were used in a week. It was Sing's prerogative to save the sacks, and he stored them up in his room. The Chinamen's room was sparsely furnished just bunks, a table and chair, a lantern and, in the corner, stacks of laundered flour sacks. We used to sit on Sing's flour sacks when we watched him write to his wife. He'd wash the sacks to get the flour out and fold them neatly and stack them all in his room and then he'd bundle them up every once in a while and send them to China.

They were for his family. They'd use them for clothing over there. You had to be in good with Sing to get a flour sack. That was his side issue.

Sing roasted all the coffee that was drunk on the ranch and that was a lot. Coffee was served with every meal and the coffee came up to the ranch on the train in big sacks like the flour. They were not cotton like the flour sacks; they were much coarser. I don't remember Sing saving any of the coffee sacks.

The interesting thing about Sing was the amount of work he'd do in a day, seven days a week, for four years in a row. And he never had a vacation, if you can believe that a man would do that. Today no one is willing to work like that and I don't blame them. In the summertime, there were as many as fifty men working at the Santa Margarita, doing all sorts of work. There'd be stablebucks, vaqueros and people running threshing machines and doing whatever work had to be done. In the wintertime it slowed down because there wasn't much work then. So, in winter, there were only about twenty men on the ranch. They all ate in a large room we called the men's dining room. It was a big room with long tables in it like a mess hall. And all these men were Mexicans or of Spanish descent, as opposed to the artisans like the blacksmith and the carpenter, who were usually of English or German descent.

Sing also had the family to feed, anywhere from six to ten or twelve people. He would have one menu for the family and another for the men. We ate a little better than the men did and we ate in a different room, the family dining room. It wasn't fancy food but it was damned good, I'll tell you that. So, there was Sing at a woodburning range—a great big thing with huge ovens. Incidentally, Sing had a helper, a Chinaman named Hom. His job was to wash the dishes and do all the scullery work. Sing and Hom had their meal, too, a Chinese meal which Sing had to cook, naturally. Of course, they ate at a different time, about four o'clock in the afternoon, and their meal consisted of octopus and other exotic foods that my mother had shipped down from San Francisco's Chinatown for them. That was it for help in cooking for all those people every day—just Hom to do the dishes and the pots and pans.

Sing's English was pretty good, but it was slightly pidgin. And he spoke Spanish quite well. He'd speak to these Mexicans and rattle on and I think he got the three languages mixed up at times. But poor old Hom never left the ranch for fifteen years. He didn't go back to China, or visit in San Francisco, or even Oceanside. And he didn't speak a word of English. I asked Sing once if Hom could speak Spanish, and Sing said 'No, and he's forgotten most of his Chinese, too.' I guess poor Hom had a pretty hideous existence on the ranch. Kind of a strange man. You'd hear Sing giving him instructions in Chinese, and Hom would work all day. I can't remember ever hearing him say a word. He just worked quietly around the ranch house and lived up in the Chinamen's room for all those years.

Although Sing never left the ranch, he had a friend living over in Oceanside named Sam Wing. We thought he was a mysterious sort of Chinaman. He ran a laundry and lived out by the railroad tracks in Oceanside next to his vegetable garden. We liked to think he was an opium smuggler or something exciting like that. Sam Wing would call the ranch house on this crank phone we had. We had a phone all the time I was on the ranch, put in before I was born. It was a private line kept up by the ranch. We could phone from the ranch house to Oceanside. Mr. Everett ran the grocery store in Oceanside where the ranch bought a lot of supplies. And when we rang the phone at the ranch, Mr. Everett at the grocery store would answer it. He could connect us with the main line to Los Angeles. And the Las Flores had a phone, and there were phones at each of the smaller houses on various parts of the ranch. At San Mateo there was a small house where Rodriguez lived with his wife and children and, when the vaqueros weren't in that area, he'd take care of the windmills and the fences and whatnot. There was a phone there in case he had to report something to the main ranch house. There was a phone at Capitan's house over at the Mission Viejo, too. If you wanted to phone Oceanside, you'd turn the ranch house crank over once. That was Mr. Everett's number, one ring. All the phones on the line would ring once and everybody would know that someone was phoning Mr. Everett's store. If you wanted Dr.

Nichols in Oceanside, he was two rings. Rodriguez at the San Mateo was one short and one long. They had tricky rings like that. Capitan's was ... I can't remember but I think it was the reverse, one long and one short. And the Santa Margarita was four rings.

Now, every once in a while, Sam Wing would come into Mr. Everett's store and he'd phone Sing. We had only one phone at the ranch house. It was out in the patio and hung on the wall on a sort of wooden box. And the phone would ring four times and it would be Sam Wing. So, you'd go off and get Sing, and Sing would stand out in the patio and, God! you could hear him talking in that sing-song Chinese all over the ranch house. Of course, we had no idea what he was talking about, but I think Sing thought he had to yell all the way to Oceanside. The louder he yelled, the better the conversation he was having. Sing never did understand the phone and nobody ever explained it to him. So, for years, Sing was trying to yell all the way to Oceanside.

Every day was a workday for Sing and it started very early. The first meal usually started about six-thirty in the morning, every day including Sundays, no vacations, and when the four years were up, Sing would go back to China. He did all the cooking, all the baking; everything that was consumed, he made it. Of course the menus in the mens' dining room were quite basic menus: meat always and frijoles and potatoes and not too much on the greens. The strange thing about the meals was that these were all people of Mexican descent, but Sing didn't cook Mexican food. He always served beans, three meals a day including breakfast. They were red beans, but not highly seasoned. They were not like you get in a Mexican restaurant now. They were just red beans with a thick sauce. Great pots of these things were always cooking on Sing's range.

He cooked mostly stews and meats ... we didn't butcher many cattle on the ranch ourselves. It wasn't worth it. They did once in a while out at the vaquero camps, but we had a train running up by the ranch house anyway, so they'd ship up sides of beef from Hardy's Packing House down in San Diego—big sides of beef because that had to feed a lot of men. They hung it up in what we called the meat room. They didn't have any refrigeration for beef but the meat room was the coolest room in the house and the meat was used too quickly to spoil. Sing had to cut it all up himself and make stews out of it and put in onions and potatoes and other things. I'm not sure about the details but there were damned few greens, I'll tell you that. Once in a while, the family would be served a salad, a very simple salad. We didn't have any choice. In those days they only grew one kind of lettuce and that was what they called Los Angeles lettuce. Now you call it head lettuce. Nobody ever heard of any other kind. Not even in San Francisco. These other kinds of lettuce have only come in the last fifty years.

We'd have bread with every meal, too. It was just regular white bread or, sometimes, biscuits and, once in a while, cornbread. Sing didn't bake every day, but he'd bake probably a couple of days a week, so the bread was always fresh. And I used to hang around him, as a child would, watching him do these things, and the cooking became very automatic with him, because it was the same recipe day after day. It never changed. The baking took time but the bread was quite good. It was maybe better than the bread we have now.

For dessert, Sing would bake pies: apple pies, apricot pies and sometimes prune pies—to keep the boys loose, I guess. He made all the pie crust from scratch, naturally. And, then, cookies—always the same kind—sugar cookies, and they were very simply made. He had a cookie cutter he stamped them out with that was always the same shape. The men got cookies, too. Oh, and the bread pudding! Bread pudding was another of Sing's big desserts. I don't know if you know what bread pudding is. In the kitchen they had these big milk pans, used to put milk in when the cowherd brought it in. We had about ten or twelve cows there that we used for milk for the family and for cooking. The cowherd would milk out at the corrals and he'd bring the milk up to the kitchen in buckets and pour it into these pans. Sing would let the milk settle in the pans and let the cream come to the top. Then he'd use a metal skimmer that looked like a clamshell to skim the cream off. And he'd take this milk and he'd add custard or something like that and lots of cinnamon and spices for flavoring. Then he'd cut up chunks of bread like croutons, about as big as dice, throw it into the pan with the milk and mix it all up. Then he'd put it in the oven and bake it for a while and, when it was done, it was like eating a custard pudding. It was called bread pudding because bread was one of the main ingredients. And that was what the men got for a sweet dessert sometimes. It was pretty good, as a matter of fact. It wasn't bad at all, but, of course, seven days a week of it got a little tiresome.

To drink with your meal, you could have coffee, tea if you wanted it, but usually coffee. Of course, the kids drank milk. But the men all drank coffee. The ranch bought coffee in sacks, hundred pound sacks. It came up on the train and the wagon would go down to the siding and haul it up to the house. The coffee wasn't roasted. The unroasted coffee beans weren't brown at all but the color of peanuts. So, Sing would have to roast all the coffee beans. He had square, flat pans and would spread out the beans on the bottoms of these pans and he'd stick them in the oven to roast. By his own timing method, he'd open the oven once in a while and pull out the pans and look at them and shove them back in again until they were dark brown. And then he'd have to grind the beans himself. There was a big grinder on the wall and he'd pour the beans into it and turn the big crank by hand. So, the coffee was all made from scratch and the reason for that was that it was too expensive to buy it any other way. But I never saw Sing drink coffee. He'd keep a cup of tea on the table by the stove—not on the stove but by the stove because he liked to drink his tea cold. I don't know if this was a common practice of the Chinese of that day but Sing would keep a cup of cold tea near him all day and he'd stop what he was doing every so often and walk over for a sip of cold tea.

We ate a little better at the family table than they did in the men's diningroom. We ate a lot of steaks. The meat we got was the best. Charlie Hardy wouldn't dare send anything to the Santa Margarita Ranch that wasn't the best he had in his packing house because Hardy was a friend of my uncle's. He'd send up these special cuts for the family table. The steaks weren't thick. People think the thicker the steak the better. They were thick, maybe an inch or inch and a half but none of these steaks thick as a roast. We'd have steak two or three times a week and other times maybe roast beef or chops. All the things that people have today. And mashed potatoes, that was standard fare, too, and always with gravy. At the family table, we had vegetables, nothing fancy, turnips or peas—par for the course for that period. And coffee or tea and pies. Apple pie or prune pie or sometimes apricot pie. His desserts were great. Sing's apple pies were really something. He baked all the pies and baked all the bread and roasted all the coffee. Looking back on it, how he did it for as long as he did is beyond me. As kids, we didn't think anything about it. We didn't have anything to compare it to anyway. So this went on seven days a week, fifty-two weeks out of the year for four years at a crack and no days off.

As kids, we thought our meals were pretty elegant, at least compared to the meals served in the men's diningroom. But, looking back on it, I don't think it would be considered elegant by today's standards, mostly because of the flies. The corrals were not far from the house and, so, there were always flies at the ranch house. In those days, we didn't have the insecticides and the bug lights they have now, so we just put up with these constant flies. Nobody thought anything of it; the flies at the ranch house were just a fact of life. The only effective countermeasure we had against the flies was flypaper, and they put flypaper everywhere; the kitchen, the livingroom, and the diningrooms. So, all through the meal, there would be the constant buzzing of flies stuck to flypaper. That was our dinner music and our centerpiece.

Sing would cook breakfast starting at about 4:30 or 5:00 every morning and then, after breakfast was over, prepare lunch for the rest of the morning. I remember there were always crews of men out maybe two or three miles from the house working in the alfalfa fields or doing some other kind of work. The stablebuck had a chest as big as a steamer trunk with a hinged top and rope handles. And old Sing would have to load that with pans of hot stew or whatever it was they were having for lunch and put it in the wagon. Off this stablebuck would go with pies and all the food to feed the men working in the fields. I used to go out with the lunch wagon as a kid, particularly if the men were working on the threshing machine. I was the boss's nephew and I guess I pestered the hell out of everybody on the ranch but they had to put up with it. It was a typical ranch wagon—a two-horse flatbed wagon with short sides around the bed. You could use it for almost anything. We would go bumping along and I would hear the tableware jangle around in the big box. They sent out enameled tin plates with knives and forks and tin coffee cups. It wasn't fancy but just practical tableware for these men to use in the fields. I don't know if the food was still hot when it got out to them.

That was usually the first lunch that Sing cooked after breakfast was over. And then, of course, he'd cook the family's lunch and serve it to us in the family room and, at the same time, serve lunch to whatever men were working close enough to the ranch house to eat in the men's diningroom. But by about one o'clock, he got off for a few hours until four, when he'd have to start cooking dinner. But he didn't take that time off, naturally, because he had me to take care of.

Before 1911 when the Chinese Empire was dissolved and the republicans took over, there was still an emperor of China, actually I think it was an empress at the time. Then, in 1911, the big revolution came with Sun Yat-sen. In 1911 he was the important revolutionary leader in China. But before the revolution, all Chinamen wore queues on the backs of their heads. It was a sign of submission to the emperor and had been for hundreds of years. Some of these queues hung down their backs like pigtails, but Sing always wore his right on the nape of his neck in a bun. When we were very small, we wanted to be as much like Sing as we could be, because we thought he was a great hero. So, sometimes, after lunch, Sing would take black shoelaces and he'd tie them around our heads and he'd braid the backs into queues. We'd run around the ranch house and play all the rest of the day with our queues on. We thought they were great. We wanted to be like Sing. But when Sun Yat-sen and the revolution came in 1911, the emperor was thrown out and the republic was established. And all the Chinamen cut their queues off, gratefully I guess. And, after that, Sing always had a regular haircut. No more queue.

These Chinese cooks were very kind people. They didn't shift around much and were apt to stay with one family for years. They became honorary members of the family. Sing had that status on the Santa Margarita because he'd been there since he was a young man and everybody was practically his contemporary. Uncle Jerome and Sing were about the same age. When he came on the ranch, Sing was about eighteen years old, Uncle Jerome was twenty and my mother was younger than both of them. Their generation was not running the ranch then. They were just the sons and daughters of the big shots and they called each other by their first names. Sing called my uncle 'Jerome' and my mother 'Minnie.' But my grandfather and grandmother were always 'Mr. O'Neill' and 'Mrs. O'Neill' to Sing. When my grandfather died and Uncle Jerome became the kingpin, it never changed Sing at all. Nobody outside the family called Jerome O'Neill anything except 'Mr. O'Neill,' except Sing. In the mornings when the family came down to breakfast, he'd say 'Good morning, Minnie' to my mother and 'Good morning, Jerome' to my uncle. That was taken as a matter of course. He was the only one who could do that and nobody asked him not to. He was accepted as a member of our family.

When my grandmother died, she was buried up in San Francisco in the family plot at Holy Cross Cemetery and they had the funeral at our home on 17th Street. I was just a young boy then, in 1916, and Uncle Jerome's chauffeur, Carl Romer, asked me, 'Where's a florist here?' I gave him the address of the florist my mother always used. Carl said 'I promised Sing I'd buy him something to put on Mrs. O'Neill's coffin.' He said that Sing had instructed him to 'buy pretty. Money I don't care, but buy pretty.'

As he told us of Sing's request, his eyes squinted with tears and his voice coughed with emotion. He was close to tears but he didn't cry. My father is a very sentimental man and will sometimes come close to crying when he is moved. What moves him most, at least what so often brings forth this upwelling of emotion is not tragedy or grief. Those are too serious and unhappy. What moves him most is the simple expression of love and affection from very special people. He sipped his drink until he regained control of his voice and, then cheerfully announced that it was late and that he had talked too much already and he thought that we should all turn in for the night.

CHAPTER FIVE

Steve Peters

Saturday morning was bright and sunny and, as Syd and I were dressing, I heard my father's voice out in the livingroom. He has always been an early riser. I didn't know how long he'd been up but he was down on his hands and knees on the livingroom rug talking to O'Banion, our dog, who was enjoying the attention. Dad must have been on his hands and knees for some time because, at his age, that was a difficult position to assume and it took him some time and struggle to get to his feet. Syd and I said, "Good morning," and went directly into the kitchen to begin making breakfast, each of us moving about our tasks in a practiced, semiconscious way. My father came into the kitchen and offered to help us, but the mere thought of having to reassign all those little tasks that go into the making of breakfast made us politely but firmly decline his offer. So, my father sat down at the breakfast table. I watched him out of the corner of my eye as I squeezed the orange juice. He used the time to study the room. He had a natural eye for design so that he noticed the aesthetic and functional allotment of space in a room: the lighting, the colors, textures—every element that produces the feeling of the place. I knew that, later on, he would tell us what he had discovered, to point out those things which affected the composition of the room.

41

At breakfast, he gave us the news of family and friends up in Atherton,
my home town, where he and my mother still lived. It was a cursory
treatment of recent events and he didn't go deeply into any of it. After
breakfast and as soon as the dishes were cleared and washed, Dad
disappeared into his room and reappeared carrying an old black
photograph album. He told us these were pictures of the ranch and we
might be interested. He sat down at the breakfast table and Syd and I took
seats on either side. He opened the album and pointed to a photograph
and said:

Now this picture is interesting because this man's name is Steve
Peters, and he was the head of the vaqueros. His last name was 'Peters'
so his father was American, I guess. In those days people never talked
about those things and I never thought to ask. But he had swarthy skin,
curly black hair and he wore a goatee and mustache, but not big ones. He
was lean—quite a nicely built man. To me, he looked like Buffalo Bill.
But he was about my uncle's age, I guess, or maybe a little older and he
had worked as a vaquero on the Santa Margarita practically his whole
life. He didn't retire until he was about seventy-something. He was
about sixty when this picture was taken. He was a magnificent horseman
and a wonderful man. And the reason I'm dwelling on him is that he was
the head of the vaqueros, the majordomo, for many, many years when
we were kids.

Steve was an unusual man. Even as a young boy I knew that. Steve had
a gentlemanly spirit about him, although I don't think he had any
education at all. He was a gentleman by nature and people knew it as
soon as they met him. They could tell it just by looking at him. He had
that way about him. He wasn't haughty but a very proud and gentle man.
He spoke Spanish softly; it wasn't particularly beautiful Spanish, just
Mexican Spanish, but it was beautiful to hear him talk. He spoke English
quite well, naturally, but with an accent. His tone was gentle except
when he was giving orders to his men. His voice was low-pitched and he
had a unusual way of addressing people, particularly if they were his
elders or his boss or if he were talking to my mother. And since he had

lived there all his life, he knew my mother and all the womenfolk on the ranch. My mother always said, "Good morning, Stephen." Everybody called him Steve, but for her it was 'Stephen.' "Good morning, Mrs. Baumgártner," always the accent on the next to the last syllable as in Spanish. He had his own room down at the adobe bunkhouse because he was the big boss. In the evenings, he'd come up to the ranch house to report to Uncle Jerome, or my grandfather, when he was alive, and get orders for the next day. And he would knock on the door to the livingroom and come in. He'd stand there with his sombrero in his hands in front of him. And he would bow to my mother and any other women who happened to be sitting there and, in a very soft voice, not timid or shy but low and quiet, he would report what he had to report; he'd receive his orders for the next day and bow to the ladies as he backed out the door.

Ambrosia Valenzuela was the head vaquero before Steve. He was short and he looked a little like Pancho Villa. I don't know how long he was the head of the vaqueros on the ranch but he had as high a reputation as a horseman as anybody in Southern California. They used to tell about how he could ride a bucking horse with silver dollars between the soles of his boots and the stirrups and he would keep them there while the horse was bucking and twisting. I don't think he actually did that, but he was the kind of man they told stories like that about. So, he was a terrific horseman and I suppose he had a pleasant personality, but not like Steve's. Ambrosia was killed in 1910. Somehow his horse ran under a sycamore tree. Dr. Balou took care of him but his back was broken and he never came out of it. Uncle Jerome was at his bedside when he died. And Steve became the head of the vaqueros.

This picture of Steve Peters is interesting because it shows the typical garb of a Santa Margarita vaquero. If it was cold he'd wear a coat, but not a fancy coat. And the coat never matched anything else he had on.

Dad broke into a laugh at Steve's utter disregard for fashion.

He usually wore a vest except when it was very hot. And a shirt that buttoned up the front like a cotton dress shirt of today, and always with

44

a bandana. The bandana was not for decoration. When you drove cattle, the dust was fierce and you could pull your bandana up around your mouth and breathe better. In many places on the Santa Margarita on hot days there were swarms of gnats in the shade of the sycamore trees and, if you rode through them, they would get into your mouth and nose if you weren't wearing a bandana. And, of course, you could wipe your brow with it, too. And see Steve's hat? None of the vaqueros wore big cowboy hats like those you see in the movies. Maybe that kind of hat was worn in Texas or Montana, but never on the Santa Margarita. Steve's hat is pretty typical. It was usually a small Stetson or some hat like that with a slight brim. You can see his reata all coiled up over the saddle horn. Apparently he'd just finished roping because normally his reata would be strapped to the other side of the saddle.

They all wore jeans, just like the jeans they have now. They were usually washed a good deal so they fit properly and, very often, they wore two pair to protect their legs if they were going to ride through brush. Sometimes they wore chaps but, if they did, they were just cowhide or leather. Nothing fancy. None of those bearskin ones they wore up in places like Montana. Those were to keep your legs warm in winter, which vaqueros of the Santa Margarita didn't need. They didn't wear chaps too often on the Santa Margarita because they were uncomfortable and cumbersome if you got off your horse, and most vaqueros would get on and off their horses quite a bit during the day.

They always wore boots, of course, but they weren't exaggerated or fancy. They were practical cowboy boots. But when I say they weren't fancy, I don't mean they didn't have stitching on the sides, because they did, but that was practical, too. Stitching stiffened the leather so that the tops of the boot didn't get sloppy, and it would also provide friction when the vaquero pinched his legs against the horse so he could ride better that way. The toes were always pointed to slip into the stirrups and the boots had high heels to hold the stirrup under the arch. It's very dangerous if the stirrup slips behind your heel, as it's very difficult to get it back under the arch and, in the meantime, you're helpless. These boots were made for riding and you could hardly walk in them. That's why cowboys always kind of walk funny, like young girls trying to walk in high-heeled shoes.

The way we were taught to ride was in the vaquero fashion which differed from the Texas way of riding. My brother, John, knows much more about this than I. But it was cattle horse riding with a Mexican saddle, not English saddle with posting, because you couldn't work cattle that way. But the California vaquero rode with a very long stirrup. You adjusted your stirrups so that, when you stood on the balls of your feet in the stirrups, your crotch just cleared the saddle by an inch or so. Just enough to give you some purchase and control. I gather some of the boys from Texas rode with a pretty short stirrup, like jockeys. We never did that. Sometimes, if the vaqueros were going to ride through thick brush or when they had to go up the canyons to drive the cattle to the rodeo ground, they would wear tapaderos. Tapaderos were leather coverings over the front of the stirrup and they protected a vaquero's feet and boots from getting cut up on thorny brush. Those fancy saddle rigs they use in parades always have tapaderos, usually covered with silver and gold, which, of course, is only for show.

The biggest fear that Uncle Jerome and all the vaqueros had was of grass fires. If a grass fire were to start, there was no way of controlling it and it would go on burning until it had burned itself out. And it was the grass that fed the cattle that was the sustenance that made the ranch go. So all the vaqueros were very careful if they smoked. Ready-made cigarettes were not on the market yet, so if a vaquero smoked cigarettes, he'd roll his own. Bull Durham was what he smoked. It was a brand of roll-your-own cigarettes that came in a little pouch with cigarette papers. On the ranch as a youngster, I would see the vaqueros rolling their cigarettes and I was very impressed. Sometimes they'd roll them one-handed while riding. So when we figured we had reached that age of development when we should try cigarettes, the first step was to learn to roll a smoke. It wasn't as easy as it is today where you can just open a pack and pull out a cigarette. You had to be somewhat accomplished to smoke back in those days. At least we thought we were pretty accomplished knowing how to roll the cigarettes so they came out right. And if you got very good—and you'd only do this in front of someone if you were very sure of yourself—you'd roll a cigarette with one hand. That was really the *pièce de resistance* for us kids. But Bull Durham at the ranch wasn't my first attempt at smoking. Like every boy who had ever read *Huckleberry Finn,* I had made my own corncob pipe and had tried to smoke it. At the same time I went barefoot everywhere and sneaked out of my room at night to dig for buried treasure and to smoke my pipe and be as much like Huck Finn as I could. So, when I got to Bull Durham, I wasn't a complete stranger to tobacco.

But fires were considered very serious stuff on the Santa Margarita and any man who did anything that could have started a fire, would be fired. There were very few grounds for firing a man on the ranch, but that was one of them. So, most of the men did not smoke much away from the bunkhouse. And when they smoked, they'd cup their hands around their cigarettes to keep the wind from blowing sparks into the grass. They did smoke from time to time at the vaquero camps and even in the saddle, but when they put their smokes out, they'd spit into the palms of their hands and then grind the cigarettes into their palms. Then they'd peel the paper away from the tobacco and let the cigarette disintegrate onto the ground and grind the tobacco into the ground with their boots. That was the careful and correct way to put out a cigarette when you were on the Santa Margarita.

Actually, I didn't do a lot of riding. My brother, John, was a top rider as a young boy and a top roper, too. He took to it very well, but ranching wasn't for me. I liked to go out with the vaqueros and live in their camps when I was in high school. That was very romantic. But, when I was little, very often I would ride with my uncle and the cattle buyer to the rodeos. For a small boy, that was quite an adventure. The cattle buyer would come to the ranch house and spend the night before a rodeo. They were all cattlemen and friends and my uncle and the cattle buyer would stay up and talk about the price of cattle and the problems they were having. We'd have to get up especially early on the morning of a rodeo. Sing would be up early, naturally, and he'd cook us breakfast. There would be Uncle Jerome, the cattle buyer, my uncle's driver, Carl Romer, and me. After breakfast, we'd all get in the car and drive out to the rodeo—Uncle Jerome and the cattle buyer in the back seat and I'd be up in front next to Carl. It was usually dark when we left the ranch house and we'd drive for a long time—or at least it seemed like a long time to a little boy. And, I guess, maybe it was, because sometimes we'd have to go clear up to the Mission Viejo. We couldn't go very fast because the ranch roads were pretty rough and it would be dark all the way. And, though we weren't going very fast, it was enough so that the wind hit you right in the face and it was cold, even in the summer. The men didn't seem to notice, but my face and hands would be numb by the time we arrived. And, by then, the sun would be up. I'd sit in the front seat of the car, my face up to the sun to warm my cheeks. By the time we arrived, the vaqueros would already be up, have cooked their breakfast and ridden up into the canyons and arroyos to drive the cattle down to the big flat rodeo grounds. It was these men who might wear chaps and tapaderos because the brush up some of those canyons was pretty thick. The vaqueros would drive all the cattle in the surrounding area down to the rodeo ground and, if we'd gotten there particularly early, I'd sit in the car and wait. Suddenly, maybe twenty or thirty cattle would come out of a little canyon on our right, driven by two vaqueros. And, then on our left, maybe twenty-five more would suddenly appear from another canyon. And what had just moments before been a big empty field was all of a sudden alive with the commotion of dust and cattle and horses and the sound of hooves and men yelling and calves bawling. It was very dramatic to me.

Then, a vaquero would lead two saddle horses up to the car and my uncle would get on one and the cattle buyer on the other. They'd put on dusters to keep their clothes as clean as they could. Then they'd ride into the herd with two 'cut-out' men right behind them. These would be the pick of the vaqueros and they'd ride the best cutting horses on that part of the ranch. I would watch them from the car and the cattle buyer would point at one steer that he wanted to buy and my uncle would nod or shake his head, depending on whether he wanted to sell that particular one or whether he thought it was too young. They'd ride right through the middle of the herd and the herd would spread out away from them as they did. And, if Uncle Jerome showed he wanted to sell a particular steer, these cut-out men would go after it. The cutting horses were trained to get on each side of the steer that was picked for slaughter and escort it out of the herd. You had to be quite a rider to do this sort of work because the horses knew their job and would maneuver that steer out of the herd on their own initiative. If you were leaning the wrong way when the horse made a sudden turn, you could be thrown down into the middle of the herd.

Cattle buyer at a rodeo.

So, the vaqueros would drive the steer out of the herd and a couple of other riders would pick him up and drive him over about a hundred yards or more and hold him there. And one by one they would come out of the herd and pretty soon maybe four or five hundred head that were sold would be in a bunch. Many times they didn't keep them in a fenced corral. Cattle aren't the smartest animals and a few men riding around them was enough to keep them together. The selection might go on for hours, sometimes a half a day or longer. It was hard, dirty work but Uncle Jerome never failed to do it. They don't do this any more. Now, the selection is much smaller and they haul them away by truck.

My father's brother, John Baumgartner, is a California rancher and, as such, is very aware of his Santa Margarita heritage. The California ranching tradition dates back to the Mexican and Spanish periods, a tradition uninterrupted by such Mexican-Anglo animosities as those of the Texas war with Mexico of the 1830's. Following that bitter war, Texans anglicized many of the Spanish ranching terms—"la reata" became "lariat" and "jaquima" became hackamore. California cattlemen have retained Spanish cattle terms and their correct Spanish pronunciation.

John had been instrumental in founding an annual rodeo in San Benito County, which our family has attended nearly every year. Before each rodeo, I was reminded of the true pronunciation of "rodeo"—ro-dá-o. The Anglicized version "ró-de-o" from Oklahoma and Texas was never used in front of my uncle or his fellow cattlemen and to do so would have been an unforgivable faux pas, even for a child. The pronunciation of rodeo is a distinction traditional California cattlemen maintain and to use the Texas pronunciation is equivalent to abandoning an honored heritage.

The cattle that were sold were driven from the rodeo grounds down to one of the shipping corrals alongside the railroad. There was a big corral at San Onofre, on the bottom land right at the mouth of the canyon, near where the nuclear reactor is now. The cattle were driven into the corrals and then, one by one, driven up the loading chutes, weighed on scales and put into cattle cars. They usually loaded about 20 animals into each car. Cattle at that time averaged about 1275 pounds. When they had a rodeo, they'd load anywhere from six to ten cars. In those days a train would bring the cattle cars up from San Diego and leave them on the siding for a day or two. When one car was full, they'd move it down seventy feet or so to get the next car in front of the chute. I can remember seeing them moving the cars along with crowbars. A vaquero would put a crowbar under the wheel and get leverage enough to move it down the line. They could 'pinch it along,' as they called it. Later on, the railroad wouldn't let them do this. It seems that this wasn't a very safe practice, because, if the men who were pinching the cars forgot to set the brakes, the car could roll onto the main line and cause a wreck. So later, the railroad would send up a locomotive to move the cars even that little distance and they had a train crew to make sure the brakes were set. The train would usually take the cattle to Charlie Hardy's slaughter house in San Diego or to the Cudahy Packing Company up in Los Angeles, a short ride.

For years, the vaqueros were busy trying to stamp out the Texas fever tick. From about 1916 to 1920, the cattle would get this particular tick that, I suppose, originally came from Texas and it was killing the cattle. It was a very serious problem for the Santa Margarita and all the ranches. We had to divide the ranch into five sections and close each section off with fences. It was very costly. There were around 25,000 head of cattle on the Santa Margarita and they all had to be dipped several times a year. In each general area there were dipping corrals, and before the cattle could move from one area to another they had to be dipped to kill any ticks they might have had. All the gates on the ranch were locked in those days and all the keys were kept in the office at the ranch house. Nobody could go through the ranch without permission. We had a full-time government veterinarian in charge of the dipping. Dr. Rosenberger was his name and he was an awfully nice guy. He and some of the men would dip the cattle in one section and move on to the next. It was a very expensive operation. As kids, we used to think it was fun to watch.

The dipping was very humane; the animals weren't hurt at all. Dr. Rosenberger would boil a big vat of oil and arsenic until it was all brown. The cattle were forced up a chute and prodded to jump into the dipping trough. These troughs were four feet wide and maybe fifteen feet long and six feet deep. The cattle would have to swim through this brown dip. There was a walkway raised about three feet along one side so a man could lead the cattle through the trough. He had a pole about eight feet long and on the end was an S-shaped bar. He'd use this pole on the cattle as they came through. If it was a full-grown steer, it would swim through, keeping its head above water. So the man would put the top part of this S hook over the steer's neck and push his head under to get any ticks that might be there. And if it was a calf who couldn't swim very well, he'd use the lower end of the S under the calf's neck to hold its head up. The cattle would go through the dipping troughs right into the drying pens and then they could graze in a new section of the ranch. They might dip 500 to 600 head a day, and this went on for years!

Dr. Rosenberger was a very kind fellow. During the summers, we liked to go out and stay with him in the vaquero camps. He liked to sing a lot of tunes like "Sweet Adeline" and other songs. We'd heard the vaqueros sing in Spanish all our lives but we'd never heard the songs Dr. Rosenberger sang. Today you'd call them folk songs and he sang them, not for our entertainment, but for his own amusement. He had a guitar and he'd strum and sing these songs at the top of his voice. I don't know how well he played the guitar or sang but we thought he was great, and, if his voice wasn't so good or his strumming wasn't too accomplished, it didn't bother him a bit. He'd put his head back and sing like he wanted the whole ranch to hear. He taught us these songs by picking his guitar very slowly and each time he picked a string we'd sing a word. He was very patient and he'd go over each song until we knew it. Then he'd strum his guitar and we'd all put our heads back and sing. It's a wonder we didn't stampede the cattle.

He chuckled at the memory and turned the page of the picture album. He mumbled about the pictures on the next few pages to indicate that they were of no real importance. And then he began to tell us about his mother's side of the family, the O'Neills, who were the owners of the Santa Margarita.

(LEFT TO RIGHT:) Uncle Dick, John, Richard O'Neill, Sr., unidentified gentleman (probably a cattle buyer), and Uncle Jerome.

CHAPTER SIX

The O'Neills

MY GRANDFATHER, Richard O'Neill, had come to the New World with his family when he was one year old. He was born in Ireland, in Mitchelstown, County Cork, and his whole family emigrated to St. Andrews, New Brunswick in 1825. St. Andrews is on the coast, right across the Canadian border from Maine. His father was a butcher and he became a butcher, too, eventually moving down to Boston. By 1849, he found that his butcher business wasn't as far along as he'd hoped, so he came out to California to seek his fortune in the Gold Rush. He tried mining for gold but that was back-breaking work and didn't yield the riches he had expected. So he moved down to San Francisco and opened a butcher shop. He had good success and when he was well established, he decided that it was time to marry and settle down. But a great many of the women who had come out West during the early days of the Mother Lode were working as prostitutes and saloon girls—women an old-world Irish Catholic like my grandfather would never consider for matrimony. So, he left his business and sailed around the Horn, back to his family home in St. Andrews. There he was introduced to another family named O'Neill. They had the same last name but were not related. They had come over in 1820 from Drumore, a small town in

County Tyrone in northern Ireland. There were four girls in the family and a strict father who guarded over his daughters so carefully that some of them never did marry. Richard O'Neill talked to the father about which of the girls he could marry, and after one of the girls rejected his proposal he married one of her sisters, Alice. I remember my grandmother, Alice, very well. She used to tell me that, as a young girl, she was living happily with her family in St. Andrews, and suddenly she was on a ship going to California with some man she didn't know. It was one of those family-arranged marriages that in today's world seems so improbable but which turned out to endure far better than many modern marriages. So, Richard O'Neill had gone back to get a wife. He got one and brought her back to California and continued his business.

My grandfather's butcher shop was located next to the Washington Market on Washington Street, between Sansome and Montgomery. In those days in San Francisco, a market was a large area under one roof filled with stalls selling fruits, vegetables and meats. Each stall was rented and operated by an independent groceryman who very likely grew, harvested and sold his own produce. People would come from all over the city to do their grocery shopping there. So, O'Neill's butcher shop was well located, right in the heart of the biggest food shopping district in San Francisco.

By the early 1860s, Washington Street had also become the site for the Mining Exchange. The Exchange was similar to the New York Stock Exchange except that it dealt exclusively in stocks of the many mining companies of the Comstock Lode in Nevada. By the 1860s the Comstock Lode had replaced California's Gold Rush as the chief driving force of San Francisco's and California's economy. Also on Washington Street and not far from my grandfather's butcher shop there was a saloon called the Auction Lunch. It was run by two Irishmen, James Flood and William O'Brien. The name of their bar was derived from the many auction houses on the block and the fact that the saloon provided its patrons with snacks along with their drinks, a common practice for saloons of the day. The Auction Lunch was a watering hole for brokers from the nearby mining exchange where they could discuss business over drinks and feast on the smorgasbord which Flood set up every morning. The usual fare was cold meats and sliced breads and Flood bought his meat every morning from your great-grandfather's butcher shop. Through this business association, they became good friends and remained so throughout their lives.

During the 1860s and '70s, the Comstock Lode became the biggest single mineral strike in American history. Millions of dollars of silver and gold were taken out of mines in Nevada, and the companies who owned these mines traded stock at the Mining Exchange on Washington Street. The real wealth of all this mining did not rest so much on the picks and shovels of the miners as on the financial maneuverings of the Mining Exchange. Many a fortune was made by men who never saw the inside of a mine shaft. The first major institution to recognize this new source of wealth and power was the Bank of California. Under the direction of William Ralston and William Sharon, the Bank of California created a monopoly which controlled the entire Comstock Lode. Historians would later call this monopoly "Ralston's Ring" and it extended to every phase of the Comstock. But the weakness of this monopoly proved to be its very size, so immense that Sharon and Ralston could not effectively oversee their entire operation.

In 1871, two Irishmen named Fair and Mackay, both experienced miners, appeared on the Comstock and determined that one of its largest mines, thought to be worthless, was, in fact, perhaps the most valuable mine yet discovered. To secure control of the mine's stock, they quietly went into partnership with Flood and O'Brien, who, by that time, had learned a great deal about the workings of the Mining Exchange from their customers at the Auction Lunch. Flood and O'Brien quietly used their knowledge to secure a controlling interest in the Consolidated Virginia Mine. Fair and Mackay proved right: the mine was fabulously wealthy. Within a few months, the Consolidated Virginia was producing a quarter million dollars of ore a month. Before the mine had run its course, it yielded an estimated $136 million, making these four Irishmen truly "the Silver Kings," the wealthiest men in the world of the 1870s. And Ralson's

Ring was smashed. No longer could the Bank of California control the Comstock, not with the formidable presence of these Irishmen and their incredible wealth. The Bank of California nearly collapsed and William Ralston committed suicide. The whole upheaval caused a serious depression in the West. And in the end, the Silver Kings founded their own bank, the Bank of Nevada, and carried out the business of banking: lending money to businesses and using property as collateral.

Among the properties mortgaged by the Bank of Nevada was the Chowchilla Ranch in the San Joaquin Valley near Merced. The owners of this 100,000-acre ranch eventually defaulted on the loan and the bank was forced to foreclose on the mortgage. Now the new owners of a failing cattle ranch, the bank directors sought a ranch manager to put the ranch back into the black. Then the bank could sell the property and perhaps realize some profit. Knowing virtually nothing about the cattle business, the bank's president, James Flood, relied on his trust in old friends and on his astute assessment of their abilities.

Meanwhile, my grandfather had parlayed his small butcher business into quite a successful wholesale meat business in San Francisco, and in so doing, he had acquired some sense of the cattle business—at least at the market end. As a wholesaler, he had gained experience buying cattle from ranches, some of them from as far away as Southern California. He was semi-retired when Flood approached him with the proposition that he become manager of the Chowchilla Ranch and put it back on its feet again for the Bank of Nevada. Your great-grandfather accepted his offer as a chance to begin a new career. He and his eldest son, Jerome, ran the Chowchilla for a number of years.

He paused for a moment to reach for a book he had brought out with the photo album—a brown, hardcover book with a half dozen bits of paper jutting out from the top, marking pages he wanted to keep handy. Then it dawned on me that he had put a great deal of thought into what he was saying, that this wasn't simply a casual reminiscence of his childhood, but a carefully thought-out presentation for the record. Up until this point I assumed that he was only vaguely aware of the presence of the tape recorder, but now I could see that he knew that everything he said was being preserved. He continued speaking as he fumbled through the bookmarkers, looking for the passage he wanted to read to us:

O'Neill learned the cattle business so quickly that, by 1879, a cattle expert, John Clay, who was travelling through the West looking for cattle properties for his British clients, said of him, 'He was a student of the cattle business and possibly he knew as much about it as any man I ever came across.' Flood's trust in the abilities of my grandfather was so well founded that by the early 1880s, the Bank of Nevada was able to sell the Chowchilla for a profit. In the process of managing the Chowchilla, O'Neill had acquired not only a working knowledge of the cattle business but a genuine love for it. His work on the Chowchilla now completed, he explored the possibility of owning and operating his own ranch.

To understand the whole picture, I'll explain to you about the Santa Margarita. The land was originally part of the lands of the San Luis Rey Mission. In the 1830s, the Mexican government took the mission lands and, in many cases, the missions themselves away from the Catholic Church. A small portion of the mission lands was to be set aside for the Indians but many of the Mexican officials who were responsible for carrying out the distribution of these lands were corrupt and, in most cases, the Indians wound up with very little, while the Mexican officials and their friends wound up with the mission lands. In this way, much of the land of San Luis Rey Mission was taken over by Pio Pico and his brother, Andres. Pio Pico was the last Mexican governor of Alta California and he gave many of San Diego's land grant ranchos to his friends and relatives. In all the confusion and corruption of distributing the mission lands, the Pico brothers became the original owners of Rancho Santa Margarita y Las Flores.

The ranch was 133,440 acres and included seven rivers and streams, twenty miles of coastline and several lakes. It was located in what is now San Diego, Orange, and Riverside counties. Eight miles inland from the coast on the Santa Margarita River, the two brothers built a beautiful adobe ranch house, still one of the loveliest adobes in California. During and shortly after the Mexican War, both brothers were away from their ranch—Pio having fled to Mexico at the outbreak of the Mexican War and Andres having served as a Mexican general in the fight against the Yankee invaders. Their brother-in-law, Don Juan Forster, took charge of the ranch in their absence. Forster was an English seaman and trader who had married Dona Ysidora Pico, Pio's and Andres' sister. Forster also owned the Mission Viejo Rancho which adjoined the Santa Margarita to the north. The Pico brothers returned to their rancho following the Mexican War, and, through poor business practices, were forced to turn to Forster for loans to cover their increasing debts. Finally, in 1864, the Pico debt became so large that Forster took over the Pico rancho and the Forster and Pico ranchos became one enormous ranch extending all the way from what is now Oceanside to El Toro Air Base. Forster immediately began the improvements that the ranch so badly needed and it soon became a profitable business again. Forster built a two-story Monterey-style house at Las Flores, near the mouth of Las Pulgas Canyon, as a wedding present for his brother, Marcus, and his new bride.

However, the Forster ranch ran into serious problems when, in the 1870s, the state of California passed a law requiring ranch owners to fence their properties. At about the same time, Pio Pico sued his brother-in-law in an attempt to recover some of his former ranch. Pico lost the suit but the expense of the legal fees plus the enormous expense of fencing the vast Santa Margarita Rancho created a debt that Forster could not overcome. He died in 1882 and his family decided to settle the debts by selling the ranch.

Richard O'Neill, at that time in the market for a ranch of his own, came down to inspect the property and found it so attractive that he immediately sought financing to buy it. He eventually turned to his old friend, James Flood, who was always looking for new investments for his considerable wealth. In 1882 the two men went into partnership to purchase the ranch from the Forsters. Flood provided the bulk of the $450,000 sale price and O'Neill became the ranch manager, his share of the ranch's earnings going to buy a half ownership in the ranch for himself. My grandfather acquired his half partnership in the early 1900s and he died in 1910. I was only seven at that time, so my recollection of my grandfather is pretty vague.

Jerome O'Neill and visiting ladies,
Viola and Chonita van der Leck of San Francisco.

After his death in 1910, his oldest son, Jerome, became both owner and manager of the Santa Margarita. When Uncle Jerome was on the ranch, he was all business. He was the big chief—the last word about everything. Everybody respectfully called him "Mr. O'Neill," except Sing, of course. Carl Romer, his chauffeur, would drive him all around to inspect the ranch. I liked to go with them in the back seat of the car. Once we were driving down the ranch road south of the Las Flores. In those days the ranch had a road parallel with the coast and running along the foothills. Later on they re-used most of that old ranch road and made it the two-lane concrete highway between Los Angeles and San Diego. It's still there; you can see it from the freeway as you drive through Camp Pendleton. Anyway, we were coming back from Mission Viejo on this ranch road and just as we approached the Las Flores, we came across three or four men cutting wild mustard alongside the road. They were inside the fence passing the mustard over to other men who were putting it into a truck. What they wanted it for I don't know. Uncle Jerome had Carl stop right next to them and he said in a friendly way 'Hello, my men. What're you doing?' 'Well, we're cutting mustard.' 'That's nice,' my uncle said to them. 'I suppose you have the permission of the owner?' 'Oh, sure we have.' Then Uncle Jerome exploded 'The hell you have! I'm the owner! Now, get the hell off my ranch!' And these men were so startled that they dropped the mustard right then and there and got in their truck and left. Uncle Jerome turned to Carl with a smile on his face and said 'Well, I guess that'll teach those guys.' So, I think some of my uncle's outbursts were calculated to get people to do what he wanted and he wasn't really angry at all. But knowing that didn't help me when it came my turn to be the object of Uncle Jerome's anger, or pretend anger.

Uncle Jerome loved my mother. She was the baby of the family, the youngest, and Uncle Jerome was particularly kind to her. And my mother held Uncle Jerome and her father in a god-like adoration that I'm sure she never felt for her husband. He was a Baumgartner and therefore always an outsider in the O'Neill family. This German Lutheran was not given much of a place among all the Irish-Catholic

O'Neills and my mother didn't help much with her over-blown respect for the men in her own family. But Uncle Jerome was very kind to my mother. He was very kind to us kids, too, but he didn't let us get away with anything and would bark at us, when my mother wasn't around. At first he'd be very subtle about it and would just talk to you. But you knew you were in trouble and it was too late to do anything about it.

I remember my mother and father bought a second-hand Buick for us kids to drive around the ranch. My father never learned to drive, but my mother did and, so that we children wouldn't borrow her car, she got us a used 1918 Buick. I don't think my uncle approved, though he didn't say anything. He thought she was spoiling us, and maybe she was. This Buick was not in great shape but it was a good car. We were driving around the ranch one summer and we'd driven out to one of the vaquero camps and had forgotten to park the car in the shade. So, Uncle Jerome drove up in his car with his chauffeur, Carl Romer, and he stopped alongside of where we were standing. 'That's your car over there, isn't it?' It was one of his rhetorical questions that let us know we were in some kind of trouble. I answered, 'Yes, it is.' 'Nice car, isn't it?' 'Yes,' I said. 'Ever have any trouble with it?' By this time, I began to dread what must be coming. 'No, none,' I said. 'Don't you think that sun's going to hurt it?' and I answered, 'No, I don't think it'll do too much harm.' Then he said, 'Where did you get that car?' I said, 'From my mother and father.' 'They bought it for you, did they?' He was moving in for the kill and I still didn't know how or why. 'Now, where did your mother get the money to buy that car?' And there it was. No way out now. This was all said in a calm voice, a conversational tone. But when I said, 'I don't know . . .' he exploded, 'God damn it, I gave it to her! Now you get that car in the shade right now!' This all took about ten minutes, but, at the end, always the whip would lash. He didn't do this all the time, but often enough so you'd remember for a long time.

He had no interest in life outside the ranch. The ranch was his domain and he spent his days checking out every detail, no matter how small. As a young boy, I'd ride in the backseat of his car when Carl drove him all over the ranch. We'd be driving along and suddenly he'd say, 'Whoa.

What's that over there?' And he'd have Carl drive over there so he could check it out, whether there was a road there or not. And not only did he have to know about the cattle business, but he had to know all about agriculture. The ranch ran cattle on the hillsides and other places suitable for grazing, but much of the bottomland and many of the mesas were very fertile, so he leased that land to tenant farmers like Aunt Jane. And he'd check on each one of these farmers to be sure they were doing all right because these people paid the ranch with their crops. If they had a crop failure, the ranch didn't get paid. So, Uncle Jerome had to know all about beans and grain and beets and when to plant and when to harvest. He constantly kept an eye on all the tenant farmers as well as all the cattle on the ranch. He was secretly very kind to these farmers. If anything went wrong and they had nothing to eat, he'd see to it that they got through it all right. But outwardly he didn't appear to be that kind of a man at all and I think that was intentional. I think he felt he had to be strong or at least appear strong and tough.

Jerome never left the ranch. I think he went to Texas once to buy some bulls and he went to New York once when he was about fifty. Other than that, he never left the ranch except on business trips to Los Angeles or to San Francisco. He would go to Los Angeles from time to time to see his lawyer, but he'd stay no more than two or three days. He had friends there and so he did have a little social life when he went to Los Angeles. And he'd come up to San Francisco three or four times a year and always stay at the Palace Hotel. Flood's main office was in the Flood building and Uncle Jerome would come up to report to Mr. Flood on ranch business. The Floods relied completely on Uncle Jerome to run the ranch. Once in a while, Mr. Flood would come down to the ranch in his private railroad car and park it on one of the ranch sidings and Uncle Jerome would report to him there. But, more often, Uncle Jerome went up to San Francisco. When he did, he would usually stay a week. He loved the theater and when he was up in the City, he'd go to the theater every night. The Palace Hotel was *the* hotel in the West in those days. No self-respecting cattleman would stay anywhere else. And Uncle Jerome would invite our whole family to have dinner with him and go to the theater. The hotel had a court in the center, covered over with a big glass canopy. It was the Palm Court of the Palace Hotel, the most famous restaurant on the Pacific Coast and we'd have dinner there and then go to the show with him. He liked that sort of thing very much.

In the meantime, Uncle Dick, Jerome's younger brother, was usually confined to the ranch. However, quite often Dick would take off on one of his escapades and no one would see him for a week or two. No one said anything while he was gone, especially not in front of us children. But when he'd been gone for a week or so and nobody knew where he was, his name would come up and everybody would hush up and my mother would sit there and look worried. If Uncle Jerome got mad at him or if he'd fallen into disfavor with any of the family, Uncle Dick would just disappear. He usually went off with some of his buddies and they'd travel around and mostly drink and play jokes on each other, some of them not so harmless. And this didn't let up even after he got married. Aunt Daisy, his wife, used to say that it was the full moon that set Dick off. He usually went to the same spots. He'd go over to Soboba Hot Springs or maybe Palm Springs and usually work his way up to San Francisco. Uncle Dick didn't have good command of the English language at times. There were some words he would never pronounce correctly. It was 'Soboba Hot Springs' but he always called it 'Suburba Hot Springs' and Palm Springs was always 'Pam Springs.' If he didn't come home on his own, then someone would be sent out to find him. When he was old enough, my older brother Richard was the one who usually was sent. One time, Richard found him in the Palace Hotel in San Francisco; he often wound up there. On the way back to Southern California on the train, Richard was talking to him about where he'd been and what he'd been doing and Uncle Dick said that he didn't remember anything except that, at one point, he found himself sitting at a banquet table in a convention of the Royal Order of Eagles and some guy was toasting a new member and the new member turned out to be Uncle Dick! He couldn't remember anything more.

At this, we all laughed so hard and I questioned the truthfulness of the story. But my father assured me that Richard had told him that that is what Uncle Dick had reported. He paused to wipe the tears from his eyes and to sip his drink and, when he felt that he could resume telling about Uncle Dick without laughing, he continued:

While Uncle Dick was very popular with the women of Los Angeles and Oceanside, he showed no inclination to marry until he finally married Aunt Daisy in 1916. Marguerite Moore was her name, but everyone called her Daisy. Her family went way back in California history. She was a direct descendant of the Sepulveda family that owned Rancho Palos Verdes. He was fifty-three at the time and Aunt Daisy was thirty-seven. It wasn't the earliest marriage that anybody ever had and the courtship was a little rocky, too. They say that Uncle Dick courted Aunt Daisy for fifteen years, but that's stretching the truth a little. Actually, they knew each other for fifteen years but the actual courtship was pretty spotty all along. During that time, Aunt Daisy spent six years in Africa visiting her sister and Uncle Dick was gone for another year on a tour of North America, escaping a breach of promise suit of some other woman. When the coast was clear, Uncle Dick came home and he and Daisy were married in 1916. I think the family put pressure on Dick to marry, hoping it would settle him down a bit. Uncle Dick and his bride moved to Los Angeles and they rarely came down to the ranch after that. Aunt Daisy was a pretty tough lady; I guess she had to be to get along with Uncle Dick. She was very outspoken. She had been raised in Los Angeles and wasn't about to go down and live on 'the farm,' as she called it and they never did. I'd go down to Los Angeles in the summers to visit them when they were first married and Uncle Dick would pick me up at the train. He was very kind to me and I'd stay at their home for three or four days. At that time they had no children and Uncle Dick would take me to the circus or the movies. I suppose I was a headache to have around but Uncle Dick seemed to enjoy entertaining me, and Aunt Daisy didn't seem to mind either.

Uncle Dick and Aunt Daisy had their first child in 1917, a year after they were married. That was Alice O'Neill, named after the aunt who had raised me at the ranch house when I was very young. I was fourteen when she was born, and she was so much younger than I that I never really got to know her. She's been living in Southern California since then and I've been in San Francisco, so we've never been geographically close and we've never had a chance to talk about her father. Uncle Dick was a wonderful guy; he was kind and generous and good-natured and funny but he was pretty wild for his time. I don't know whether Alice ever saw that side of him. He would have been sixty-three by the time she was ten and even Uncle Dick had slowed down a bit by then.

After my grandfather died in 1910, the family battle that I alluded to earlier erupted. I really don't know much about it because Victorian families, at least our family, never talked about problems like that, particularly not in front of the children. But, in my grandfather's last year, he was not too aware mentally and apparently John McDade had tried to get him to sign a paper giving the McDades a greater share of the ranch than the other children. I'm sure Aunt Alice didn't have a hand in it, but she was married to him. McDade was tossed out of the family one hundred per cent. Uncle Jerome ordered him off the ranch and as John McDade was about to step up into the buckboard to leave, he turned to Uncle Jerome and offered his hand. Uncle Jerome stiffened and turned his head to one side, completely dismissing the gesture. Aunt Alice started to cry and McDade drove off. Aunt Alice stayed on at the ranch for a few days. She had to choose between her husband and her family. She elected to be loyal to her husband and so she was out in the cold, too.

The O'Neills gave the McDades the house on 17th Street and none of the family ever saw or spoke to Alice again. It was one of those stupid things that happens in families sometimes. For the first six years of my life, Aunt Alice had raised me like a mother and she was a wonderful woman, but she had a lousy husband.

Our family was living in the 17th Street house in San Francisco when all this happened and, when the O'Neills gave the McDades this house, we abruptly moved across town to live in Pacific Heights. My brother John and I still had friends living in the old neighborhood, and on Sundays we were allowed to take the streetcar back to play with them and even visit with Aunt Alice. And we did that for more than a year. It was okay if we went to see Aunt Alice, but when we came home, nobody asked us how she was or what she was doing or anything about her. It was as if she had ceased to exist, and this went on for years, until 1928.

CHAPTER SEVEN

Children at the Ranch House

My father looked down at the forgotten photo album lying on the table in front of him. He had taken a sidetrack from the photos he was showing us, but now he continued his original direction:

Here are some cute pictures of us kids on the Santa Margarita. This one is of John and me over by the corrals, playing with some lumber. Apparently the carpenter was building something and we had appointed ourselves his apprentices.

When I lived on the ranch, I would spend my days playing around the ranch house because there was no other place to go. When John was living there too, we would play together and there were a few things we particularly liked to do. In the morning after breakfast, we would play in the barn and around the barnyard. We'd pretend to be vaqueros and we'd rope the smaller pigs with our reatas, pretending they were cattle. When we played vaquero, we'd rope anything that moved and sometimes we would rope one of the dogs. There were a lot of dogs around the ranch. The vaqueros had a few down at the bunkhouse and we had two house dogs, a cocker named Duchess and Toro, a bull terrier. Duchess was a

little on the timid side and as soon as she saw the reatas in our hands, she'd take off for the protection of Aunt Alice or Auntie Wee up at the Ranch House. We didn't usually rope the vaqueros' dogs because we were a little afraid of them. So we roped Toro if we could. He seemed to like it and treated it as the game it was. Aunt Jane and Auntie Wee didn't like this particular activity because when we'd come up to the house for lunch, we'd be very dirty, covered with dust and mud and hay. They'd have to stop what they were doing to wash us up and maybe see that we changed our clothes. And during our Saturday night baths, the women would mutter about all the fleas we'd picked up roping the pigs. But they never told us not to rope them because I suppose it kept us busy doing something we enjoyed and they didn't have to look after us.

Another of our favorite games was to ride around the barn in a goat cart we had. The goat cart was just an old piece of shelf and someone had put the wheels from my sister Bessie's old baby carriage on it. The harnessmaker had made us reins and a harness that we could hook up to our white donkey named Donkey Dan and he would pull the cart for us. Donkey Dan was a lot easier to steer than the goats because he would respond to the reins. We couldn't train the goats to the reins so we were pretty much at their mercy. They'd just walk where they liked, pulling us behind them. We didn't mind because we were just playing and we had no where in particular to go. We use to ride our pony around the ranch house, too. They kept a fine little pony named Valentine in the barn for

John and Jerome roping pigs.

71

Richard, John, Jerome, and Bessie.

us kids to ride, but the adults always supervised that so we couldn't just go down and ride by ourselves.

In the patio at the ranch house, we had a pet raccoon for a while. I think it was Carl Romer's pet. Carl was Uncle Jerome's chauffeur and lived in a room at the main ranch house and he seemed to be in charge of the raccoon. This raccoon would get up on your lap and stick his paws in your pockets looking for food. If you let him, he'd take everything out of your pockets—pick them clean. I don't think the raccoon was around for very long. Carl and one of the vaqueros started worrying that it might run away and they decided to neuter it and put it on a chain. So,

72

they got a kitchen knife and fixed it right there in the patio and put a chain around its neck and tied the chain to the bougainvillea that grew in the patio. But within a few days he was gone and Carl couldn't find him. Apparently the raccoon had pulled his chain off the bougainvillea and dragged it away, climbed one of the orange trees and fell off, hanging himself. One of the vaqueros found him and, though it was a tragedy of minor proportions to us kids, the men made a joke of it, saying that the raccoon was so disgusted with his life after he'd been fixed that he had committed suicide.

Once a year a few men would be sent over to Anaheim in the wagon to buy the wine that was to be drunk on the ranch throughout the year. In those days Anaheim was all vineyards and there were two or three large wineries up there. The men would come back with big barrels of red wine. During the year all the empty bottles were saved, and the day before the wine barrels were brought in, all the bottles were washed so that the wine could be transferred from the barrels to these bottles. Then it was put on the dining table for the men and the family to drink during meals. No one at the table was supposed to drink much of this wine. It was just something to drink with your meal and nobody ever abused the wine supply, at least not that anybody noticed. At the family table, we drank very little wine. The family members weren't big drinkers at all, but the men might have a glass or two. The ladies didn't drink at all unless it was Christmas or some very special occasion. But when these wine casks came in from Anaheim, two or three ranch hands would be selected to pour the wine from the barrels into the bottles, and they weren't supposed to, but they always did sip wine as they worked. I think filling the wine bottles was a job very much sought after.

By the afternoon, these men would be swaying and lurching around the patio as they worked. The women in the ranch house pretended not to notice but eventually the men would get louder and louder and they would laugh and drop the bottles until someone was sent out to take them down to the bunkhouse and put them to bed. The next year different men would be picked, hopefully more responsible than last year's, but always by late afternoon they would have to be put to bed too.

73

Nobody in the family seemed to notice much. They didn't approve of these men getting drunk, but I think they just looked the other way for one afternoon. It was sort of expected and I think filling the wine bottles was an unspoken reward or celebration that had become part of the ranch's routine.

This is the threshing machine used during the harvest season on the Santa Margarita. When I knew the men were working the harvester in the fields, I wouldn't go fishing after lunch. I'd hitch a ride on the lunch wagon when it took the noon meal out to the men harvesting grain. I especially liked to watch the grain harvest because I was fascinated by the huge threshing machine. This was in the days before tractors and there were 100 work horses as well as 120 saddle horses on the ranch to do whatever work had to be done. This threshing machine was drawn by 32 to 42 horses and the threshing action was powered through gears off the main axle. The big paddlewheel that cut the grain they called the header and it stuck out on the right side of the harvester. The headerman stood on a wooden platform in front of an iron wheel that looked like a hand brake on a railroad car. He controlled the height of the header by turning this wheel. The grain stalks were knocked off and carried into the harvester on an endless canvas belt where the stalk was separated from the grain. The chaff would be exhausted to the rear and fell back into the field and the grain dropped into a hopper. There was always a sackman who would hold a burlap sack beneath the hopper until it was filled with grain and then he'd pass it over to two sack sewers who would sew up the sacks with needle and thread. Then the sacks were dropped on the ground to be picked up by a wagon later. All of these men worked riding aboard this huge threshing machine. It was a fascinating sight for a young boy—this enormous team and the huge machine moving through the grain field like a steamboat with all her crew working on deck.

To me the real star of this show was the man who drove the team of horses. He sat on a seat at the end of a long beam jutting out from the front of the harvester at a forty-five-degree angle. There were boards nailed along the top of this beam like a ladder so he could get up to his seat. Up there he'd be fifteen feet ahead of the harvester and eight or ten feet above the ground. The first row of horses closest to the harvester's front wheels were called wheel horses and there were usually eight. The row in front of the wheel horses had less and each successive row had fewer horses than the row behind so that the team was triangular in shape. The very front row had only two horses and these were the lead horses. The driver had two reins to control all these horses and the reins went only to the two lead horses. Driving one of these big teams was highly specialized work and the drivers were magnificent to watch. They'd guide their teams on a path through the grain that was as straight as a surveyed line. You could stand at the end of a row and look down the grain that was still standing and you wouldn't see so much as an inch of wave. Before they started harvesting, they'd take down the fences at each end of the field so that the harvester could turn around at the end of each row. It would have to turn a square corner because to turn in an arc would have taken as much time as harvesting a whole row. There were usually adjacent fields, and if they just let the horses walk into an arcing turn they would trample the crops in the other fields. So, when the harvester reached the end of each row, the driver would pull on the reins and crack his whip. Very often, he'd have a coffee can filled with stones right behind his seat. He could control the lead horses with the reins, but if one of the other horses acted up the driver would reach behind him and get one of these rocks to throw at the misbehaving horse. Some of these horses were maybe fifty or sixty feet from the driver and that was the only way he could reach them. I never saw a driver miss a horse or hit the wrong horse. But at the end of a row, the driver would crack his whip and tug on the reins and the whole team would sidestep like soldiers on parade. It was a magnificent thing to watch. The lead horses would have to take big sidesteps because they had farther to go than the others. The wheel horses would hardly move at all and the rows of horses between them would sidestep at different speeds. And one man controlled all these horses. He was more romantic to me than the engineer of a train. He was like a king sitting up on his perch and moving this heavy machine with all the men behind him working at their jobs and all the horses in front of him at his control. Of course, now it's all done by tractor, but it was a beautiful sight and at the time nobody thought anything about it. That was just the way it was done.

Often after lunch I would go with Sing up to the lake fishing. But, if I stayed around the ranch house, I'd find something to do until it was time for the train to come. The ranch wasn't as isolated as ranches and farms in other parts of the state or the West because we had a train that ran quite close to the ranch house. When the Santa Fe built the railroad, the Santa Margarita gave them an easement through the ranch for about twenty miles. I don't think the Santa Fe paid the ranch any money for their right-of-way, but they put sidings where the ranch could load cattle and the railroad agreed to run cattle cars up to these sidings when the ranch needed to ship cattle. But, meanwhile they ran a train every day from Fallbrook to Oceanside. It was good for the people of Fallbrook, because in those days it was their only link to the coast. So the train would go down to Oceanside in the morning and then run south along the coast for a few miles and leave the mainline, heading inland for Escondido. In the afternoon it would reverse itself. Every afternoon the train would leave Escondido and stop in Oceanside to pick up any mail and freight for the ranch and Fallbrook. Then it would head back to Fallbrook, stopping at the ranch to deliver mail and freight. So at the Santa Margarita we could take the train in the morning to Oceanside, do some shopping and catch the afternoon run back to the ranch house.

It really wasn't much of a train. I don't think the Santa Fe made any money on this little spurline, so they used old and outdated equipment. It was what they called a combination train. They used old, old locomotives. They didn't have balloon stacks—they weren't that old, but they were the next thing to it. They were pretty worn out and they didn't go very fast, but they did the job. There was no particular schedule the train had to keep. It was the only train on the line. They just had to get on and off the mainline at Oceanside to be out of the way of trains coming down the coast. The engine would usually pull only two or three cars, sometimes maybe just one. It was half express car and half passenger car. The front of the car was a baggage car where they carried the mail and freight and the other half was a passenger car with old wooden seats and oil lamps hanging from the ceiling. The car was probably new in 1880 or along in there and the lamps were probably used back then, but this train never ran at night so I never saw them lit. There was a little iron stove in the passenger side but it never got cold enough to light it or at least I don't remember ever seeing a fire in it.

Like all kids I loved trains, so every day when the train came in it was a great event for me. It would stop about a quarter mile from the ranch house and I usually walked down there, or very often I'd go down on the ranch wagon. They always sent the wagon down to load the supplies that came in and take them back to the ranch house. The Santa Margarita Station was a platform about twenty feet wide and it ran along the track for about seventy feet. There was a little building there to protect freight from the rain. We called it a station but really it was just a platform by the track. I used to wait at the station for the train because I liked to talk to the fireman and the engineer. The whole train crew was pretty old, too, and I guess they were close to retirement, seeing their last working days out on this short run. They were the same crew year after year so I got to know them all very well. The engineer's name was Al, I remember, but I can't remember the name of the fireman. The conductor was called Judge and he always wore a cap and a blue coat with brass buttons. And the brakeman was Fox. They would let me climb up on the locomotive and once in a while they would say to me, 'Well, come on, boy. Hop aboard.' I'd stand on the first step and hang on to the handrail and the train would start rolling toward Fallbrook. It went down the track about a block and a half before crossing the Santa Margarita River on the trestle. There were a lot of willows around the river bank and they'd slow way down there and let me off. Then I'd walk back to the ranch house along the river.

When I didn't ride the train to the trestle, I'd get to take the mailsack back to the ranch house. There was a special sack for the ranch and every day the train would bring it from Oceanside and they'd just throw it down on the platform. It was a canvas bag with leather at the top and bottom and had a little padlock on it. The only people who had a key were the postmaster of Oceanside and the bookkeeper at the ranch house who kept the key in his office desk. The ranch got quite a bit of business mail and a lot of mail came in for the vaqueros from Mexico. So, as a kid, I was a very proud to carry the mailsack up to the ranch house. And the train crew always treated me as if I were the stationmaster of the Santa Margarita Station. I liked to think that was one of my duties. I wanted it to be my responsibility to meet the train each day and make sure that the mail got up to the ranch house so the vaqueros would get the letters from their families. That mail was important to them and I thought delivering the mailsack was one of the most important things anyone could do for them.

But the fun for the train crew came in winter when the ducks would come in and land on the ponds along the banks of the Santa Margarita River. Once the train left the mainline at Oceanside and started up the Santa Margarita tracks toward Fallbrook, they didn't have any particular schedule to keep. It didn't make any difference if they were fifteen or twenty minutes late coming into the Santa Margarita Station or into Fallbrook. They ran along the river all the way from Oceanside to the ranch house. So, in the winter they always carried a couple of shotguns in the cab of the locomotive. As soon as they got a few miles from Oceanside, they'd stop the train and get off and shoot some ducks to bring home to their families for dinner. During the rest of the year, I could see the train coming around the point down in the valley and I'd have plenty of time to walk down to the station to meet it. But during the winter, I would be playing around the ranch house and hear 'BANG! BANG! BANG!' and I'd know without even looking that the train was somewhere around the point.

They had company at the ranch house from time to time, even in the horse and buggy days. Because of the spur line from Oceanside to Fallbrook, people came up on the train. One time there were ten or twelve people up from Oceanside. On the ranch everything was very Victorian, very proper and some things were never discussed, particularly with ladies present. I think this sort of Victorian attitude

79

hung on in isolated places like the ranch long after city people had given it up. But a group of visiting ladies were all congregated in the garden for tea, discussing the latest news. One of the ladies had to go to the bathroom and they told her where the outhouse was and she sneaked away when nobody was noticing. In the Victorian period, you weren't supposed to notice when people went off to the bathroom. She went down through the gate to the outhouse. There was a latch on the door and you had to open it with a key. The outhouse was kept locked because they didn't want any of the help using it. That one was for the family and there was another one down by the barns for the hands. So, ours was kept locked and the key was hung on a leather thong in the hallway. If you had to go to the john, you got the key from the hallway on your way out. They had forgotten to tell her about the key and, when she found the outhouse locked, she waited around for a few minutes. Nobody came to her rescue so she gave up and went back to the patio and sat down with the rest of the ladies. After a few minutes, she thought she'd give it another try and as soon as an opportunity presented itself, she sneaked off again. The door to the outhouse was still locked and she returned to her seat in the patio. The sculleryman, Hom, used to help Auntie Wee in the garden and he was hoeing there in the garden that afternoon and had watched this lady come down to the outhouse several times, try the door and leave. He could see she needed help, so he went into the hallway and got the key and took it out to this group of ladies. He leaned over the lady and, with the key held out, said very clearly, 'Missy, you makee go shitty-shitty?' Can't you see these proper Victorian ladies all sitting there when this was said? They damned near dropped dead.

By about one o'clock every afternoon Sing got off for a few hours until four, when he'd have to start cooking dinner. He liked to take us fishing.

We had a lake about a mile and a quarter above the ranch house. It was a reservoir, actually, a half a mile long and about a quarter of a mile wide. It had a dam across it and it had been there for years. It was used to water the crops and was stocked with black bass. The river that flowed right by the ranch house had minnows in it that we used for bait. After lunch I'd get my bucket and wade around in the river catching minnows. Then Sing and I and sometimes my brother John, but mostly me and Sing, fishing poles on our shoulders, would go up to the lake. We didn't fish like technical fishermen. Our fishing poles were just long bamboo poles with line tied on the ends. We'd have a cork on the line and if the cork went down, you'd pull the fish out. Maybe we'd get two or three fish and turn around and tramp back to the ranch house in time for Sing to cook dinner. That didn't happen every day but it happened a great many days.

Sing liked children and he became a second nursemaid. Nothing was too good for the children. He was very kind to us, extremely so. One time, Sing and I went fishing up at the lake. I remember walking all the way up that dusty road on my own feet. Sing probably carried me back but I had walked up all by myself, so I was probably about five years old. There was high grass all around the lake and little gullies came down to the shore. And I got caught with a little diarrhea. Not only that, I dirtied my pants and kind of messed up everything. Sing took me up into one of these little gulches. We didn't have any handkerchiefs or anything so he got grass and cleaned me up the best he could and I started to cry and he said, 'That's okay, Jomie Boy. You just make some pumpkin pie.' So we went home and it was just one of those things Sing never forgot. He left the ranch in 1919 and by this time I was sixteen or seventeen. Every once in a while, he'd say, 'Jomie Boy, you remember the time you make pumpkin pie at the lake?' And everybody would say, 'Make pumpkin pie at the lake?' It was just between us and I never lived that one down. He'd always bring it up.

The customs we had at Christmas time on the Santa Margarita were very normal American traditions. Because we were on an isolated ranch they were probably somewhat different from customs other people had at that time. The children on the ranch were so removed from other families and children that our Christmas customs, particularly those that centered around Santa Claus, were carried on longer than in most families. We kids believed in Santa Claus longer because we had no one to tell us different. My father and mother would come down from San Francisco to be at the ranch house for Christmas. Aunt Jane and the Magees would come over from the Las Flores. Christmas for us kids would not be just Christmas day but would start several days before. During these days of holiday celebration, the family's Christmas traditions were carried out by the adults and they seemed to enjoy it as much as we did. Christmas at the Santa Margarita was in the German fashion rather than the English. Why that was I don't know. It wasn't only that my father was German. He wasn't very often at the ranch. And those people who lived year 'round at the ranch and who dictated the way Christmas was celebrated were mostly Irish. But, even though their names were O'Neill and Magee, Christmas was more German than English.

We decorated the house with holly. The vaqueros would ride out and bring in the holly, and I suppose they brought in the tree, too, but we didn't see that until Christmas morning. The women would help the kids decorate the house with this holly and it was part of the big buildup to Christmas.

Santa Claus was the spirit that Christmas was centered around and about a day or two before Christmas, we would all meet in what we called the big room, my grandmother's room. There was a fireplace there and that was the place we usually gathered in the evenings. So, a day or two before Christmas, we would gather in the big room and my mother or my grandmother would read us Christmas stories. All of a sudden the window blinds would burst open and there would be Santa Claus, leaning in the window with a beard and red suit and a great big book, probably a ledger from the ranch office. The ranch house walls were all made of adobe and so were very thick, which made quite a shelf for Santa Claus to use on this part of his Christmas visit. He'd open this big book and he'd have a pencil in his hand and he'd say to my brother, 'John, have you been a good boy this year?' And John would say, 'Oh, yes.' And Santa Claus would look in his book and turn a few pages and say, 'Well, yes, I guess you have,' and write down something in the book. And he'd go through each of us like this. We'd all be scared, shaking in our boots. This was real to us. This was to find out if we were going to get any presents. But, after a few minutes, he'd get through this inquisition and his head would disappear from the window and the blinds would slam shut. Then, we'd hear jinglebells as Santa's sleigh rode off. They had those jinglebells from St. Andrews, New Brunswick, and someone would be outside the window ringing them. And we could hear Santa's sleigh going off into the distance. I suppose it wasn't as realistic as we thought it was. The next morning, John and I would go out and we'd see the tracks of the sleigh in the mud. Of course they were wagon tracks but we were sure they were sleigh tracks. My older brother Richard had been to school in San Francisco by this time, so he was wise to all of this. Richard would say, 'Did you see the tracks the sleigh left?' There was nobody to tell us there wasn't a Santa Claus, so we believed this stuff until we were older than most kids. Later on in life, I was told Santa Claus was usually Ambrosia Valenzuela, the head vaquero, at least some years. Other years it might be Billy Magee or Uncle Dick. It was an honorary duty for the men on the ranch to play Santa Claus, so it changed from year to year.

The next morning, we'd all congregate out in front of the door to the livingroom where the tree and the presents were. But you couldn't go in there until everything was ready. And then the door would fly open and you could see the tree with the candles all lit and the presents and the fire burning. That was the most beautiful part of Christmas for me. Everything was a buildup to that moment. When they opened those doors, that was the real beginning of Christmas. In later years, when I was still young but no longer believed in Santa Claus, that moment still excited me. Every year I would think that that scene with the candles burning on the tree and the presents and the fire in the fireplace was so beautiful and the next year I'd be afraid that it wouldn't be beautiful any more. But it always was. It was quite a sight. And that was Christmas morning. Santa Claus always brought Christmas, everything having to do with Christmas: the tree, the presents. We decorated the house with holly but he did the rest.

We didn't go to mass at San Luis Rey on Christmas day because it was just too far to go. Most of the presents were unwrapped in the morning but then there was the big dinner in the evening. There might be fifteen or twenty people coming for dinner. Maybe Cave Couts would come over from the Guajome Ranch and the rest of the Magees from the Las Flores and some friends from Fallbrook. And they would have another Christmas present giving for the adults that arrived. The kids would be there, naturally, and there would be a few presents for us but mainly it was for those guests who had come to dinner. There would be jinglebells again and the door to the livingroom would fly open and Santa Claus would appear. He would be dressed in a Santa Claus suit and he would come and stand by the tree and give presents to everybody. The kids would stand as close to Santa Claus as they dared, scared to death, or at least very nervous. And we always had our reatas with us. This was part of the tradition. How that got started I'll never know. It had nothing to do with a German tradition or English; it was purely a Santa Margarita tradition. When the presents were all given out, Santa Claus would make a dash for the door and be gone for the rest of the year. He'd run out into the patio and we'd dash out swinging our ropes, trying to rope him before he got away. He'd run down the main hall and then out the front door and down toward the barn. Of course, the adults would try to get in our way so we couldn't catch him, and we never did. We were only five or six years old, I suppose.

The last year we did all of this, Uncle Dick was going to play Santa Claus. We were getting pretty wise by this time and I suppose my brother Richard had told us what really happened. But we didn't know who Santa Claus was and Uncle Dick pulled off the act pretty well until it came to the part where he had to run out the door. He and Billy Magee had had a couple of drinks during the present giving, so Uncle Dick couldn't run too well. And I suppose we were older and faster. Billy Magee was trying to keep us from catching Uncle Dick as he ran through the hallway. We were getting pretty close to him and Billy yelled out, 'Run, Dick, run like hell!' And that was the end of Santa Claus for us. We knew who Santa Claus was after that. But the Christmas roping of Santa Claus was very pleasant for us kids and it was very different.

The rest of Christmas was just like everybody else's. We had dinner with the usual turkey and pumpkin pie with all the people who had driven over from the Guajome, Las Flores and Fallbrook. It was a big day and it was a long trip for them. Christmas dinner was probably early in the afternoon because they had to drive home afterwards. Some of them stayed the night, but not all of them. It all seemed later in the day to us kids I suppose because we had been so excited. For days the adults had been making Christmas so pleasant and exciting for the children that by Christmas afternoon we were very tired, and after Christmas dinner we peacefully and happily went to bed early.

He paused here, not as if he intended to go on but as if he was through for the time being. Syd took the opportunity to say: "It's almost noon. I should make us all some lunch."

My father looked at us in amazement and joked: "I do go on, don't I? I've taken up the whole morning with my chattering. Now it's time for lunch and we haven't even left the breakfast table! The same thing happened the last time I talked to Louie Magee." I thought he was going to start on a story about Louie Magee but he was just laughing at himself.

Lunch came and went and, afterward, we took O'Banion for a walk in a nearby park. It was a bright, beautiful day with a soft breeze and a comfortable crispness which, for Santa Barbara, is autumn's weather. The park is a lawn-covered stretch of blufftop overlooking the yacht harbor and ocean. My father's step wasn't as long or as spry as ours. He had been slowing down for some years, I guess, but I hadn't noticed. Now, I did. He was getting old and his struggle to keep pace brought a worried look to his face. We slowed our pace imperceptibly and we walked on.

I knew what we would do for the rest of the afternoon. The University of California Golden Bears were playing football on television and, as soon as we got back to the house, we sat down to watch. My father had gone to Cal in the twenties and, when I was growing up, every fall Saturday that the Bears were playing in Berkeley, we would be at Memorial Stadium to watch them. It was our tradition, something we enjoyed doing together. Though our livingroom lacked the color and excitement of the stadium, we enjoyed the game. I don't remember if Cal won. They seldom did, but the enthusiasm we shared was enough. Just before dark, I laid a fire, Syd put a roast in the oven and we all sat down for cocktails. My father had brought out some faded typed sheets of paper, all stapled together. He started by saying:

In every family there are heroes, people who have done courageous things in small ways. But the story of what they've done is often lost down through the generations. Your great-grandmother was such a person and my father wrote down her story so that it would pass on.

He patted the front pocket of his Pendleton shirt and muttered his annoyance at losing his glasses. He searched his pants pockets and finally discovered his glasses on the sidetable next to his drink. They were half-lens reading glasses, and when he put them on he pushed them down his nose so that he could look down at the papers in his lap without craning his head forward. He began reading the history of the Baumgartner family:

CHAPTER EIGHT

Grossmuter

AFTER EACH war there has been a great wave of migration from Germany. Until the end of the nineteenth century the migration was primarily to the United States. After the revolution of 1848 in Germany there was a great exodus of young Germans to America, the land of opportunity and liberty. Christopher Baumgartner and his wife, two sons and a daughter came to Milwaukee to settle among the large community of German immigrants in that city. One son and a daughter remained in the old home near Eisenach in the western part of the Thuringian Forest. In Milwaukee one son, also named Christopher Baumgartner, soon found employment as a cabinetmaker with the Chicago, Milwaukee and St. Paul Railroad, now known as the Milwaukee Road.

Another German family left their home in Bavaria in the spring of 1854, en route to Milwaukee via New York and Chicago. John Rau and his wife, Frederieka and their three-year-old daughter boarded a sailing vessel that would take them on the first leg of a journey which would eventually reunite them with relatives in Milwaukee. But the ship ran into disastrous storms which blew the ship so far off course that it ultimately landed in New Orleans rather than New York. Not having enough money to reach their intended destination, the Rau's settled temporarily in New Orleans so that Henry could earn enough money to continue on to Milwaukee. However, Henry Rau soon took sick with yellow fever and died. With the help of some kind people, Frederieka and her daughter were put on a Mississippi riverboat and they continued their trip to Milwaukee alone. After only a few day's travel, the little girl died of the same fever and the riverboat paused long enough on the Arkansas shore for the child to be buried. Then, on the boat between St Louis and Cairo, Illinois, Frederieka gave birth to a baby boy, Henry. The only attendant she had at the birth was an old black woman who acted as midwife for this immigrant woman who spoke no English. Eventually Frederieka and her son arrived in Milwaukee and settled in with her brother Fredrick. There in the course of time she met and married the cabinet maker, Christopher Baumgartner. They had ten more children, five boys and five girls. John Baumgartner was the fourth child in the family.

My father had finished reading the little history his father had left and put it aside, took off his reading glasses and continued the story in his own words:

This John Baumgartner I'm referring to was my father, your grand-father and it was his father who built a home at the corner of Tenth and Wine streets and moved his family into it within a year after my father was born, 1865, the last year of the Civil War. The fifteen years following the Civil War were very hard times in America, but there was no dole, no bread lines. Everybody worked, glad to get seventy-five cents a day. There were no luxuries but plenty to eat. My father grew up during these difficult years. At the age of thirteen he graduated from grammar school and took a series of jobs, all of which brought out an artistic talent which he would develop throughout his life. His first job as a painter was lettering on river boat cabin doors and then he moved on to painting Victorian scrollwork on the interiors of railroad cars. Then came a job painting background scenery for theaters. In the meantime, his brother Gus had moved out to Oakland, California, where he was experimenting in the new business of canning fruits and vegetables. My father developed sinus problems which became increasingly bothersome, and in 1893 he moved out from Milwaukee to live with his brother. He hoped that the California weather would clear up his sinus condition.

You've heard of the Chicago Exposition of 1893? He had gone to that before he left for California, and when he arrived here, San Francisco had decided to have a world's fair of its own, but on a smaller scale. So they had what they called the Mid-Winter Fair in the winter of 1893-94. And it was a fair much smaller than the Chicago extravaganza, but for the West of those days it was a pretty big deal. It was held in Golden Gate Park and they had temporary buildings and the usual Ferris wheels and merry-go-rounds. There was a building where the food products of each California county were represented. Uncle Gus had a booth in the food products building where he hoped to promote these new canned olives. In his booth he had tables and chairs where people could sit and watch everybody at the fair promenade by. And Uncle Gus had a big bowl of these olives and he would hand passers-by olives on toothpicks and encourage them to sit, eat his olives and read some literature promoting his olives. My father was new in California and on Sundays he would come out to the fair and help Gus run his booth. One Sunday two very charming girls stopped by the booth and Uncle Gus gave them olives and talked with them for a minute. And when they left, my father asked who they were and Gus said 'Why, that's Mrs. McDade and her sister, Mary O'Neill.' Aunt Alice was about ten or twelve years older than my mother who, at that time, was in her early twenties. I guess my father thought my mother looked pretty good eating an olive because he made a point of being at the booth on the next Sunday when they came by again. He began a romance with my mother over this olive business and they were married in 1897 in the drawing room of the O'Neill house on 17th Street in San Francisco. Because my Uncle Gus and my Uncle Fred lived in Oakland where my father felt more at home, my mother and father rented several different houses there when they were first married. And my brother Richard was born there and Bessie and John and I was born there too.

When I was three months old my mother took me to the Santa

Margarita to live with my brothers and my sister. I lived there until I was six years old and had to go to school. Then I was shipped back to San Francisco and lived with my family and went to grammar school. I spent nearly every summer and Christmas vacation on the ranch until I went to college. In the meanwhile, in the spring of 1912 while I was still in grammar school, my father took the whole family on a tour of the United States. One of the primary purposes of the trip was to introduce us to all those relatives we had in Milwaukee. I was only nine years old at the time and don't remember too much, but I do remember meeting my grandmother. By that time she was a very old lady sitting quietly in her chair. My father said, 'This is your grandmother,' and pushed me toward her. I was a little shy, but I walked up to her and didn't quite know what to do. For a moment it was awkward, but then she put her hand up and patted me gently on top of the head and said, 'Gutes Kind, gutes Kind.' This was the woman who had come up the Mississippi to Milwaukee on the riverboat and she had been living in Milwaukee for nearly sixty years and hadn't learned a word of English. She said some more things to me in German. Under the circumstances I should have been even more ill at ease, but she had such a kind face and pleasant smile that I understood the feeling in her voice and felt comfortable. It wasn't until years later that I was old enough to understand all that she had been through and how difficult her life had been coming to the New World. She had lost her husband and child during the trip and travelled all alone up the Mississippi River in a foreign land where she didn't speak the language and she had given birth to a child on a seat on a riverboat. When I was old enough to understand all that, I felt a respect, almost a reverence for her. She was my ancestor and she was quite a woman and I felt proud and still do. Yet, when I was nine and I was standing there in front of her, all I could feel was my shyness and my awkwardness. That's the trouble when you're very young. You don't have the capacity to understand what people mean to you. As you grow up, you gain this understanding, but by that time often these people are gone.

CHAPTER NINE

The Magees

My FATHER rose stiffly from his chair and went to his bedroom for a fresh pack of Lucky Strikes, while Syd went to the kitchen to check on the roast. I put a new tape in the tape recorder. Soon we were all seated again in front of the fire, the photo album from the morning having replaced the faded pages of the Baumgartner family history on my dad's lap.

Well, let's see if there any other pictures in here you might be interested in.

This picture is a good likeness of Aunt Jane Magee. The Magee family was a very interesting bunch and they were very close to our family. Some of the details of their family history are a little vague because it was handed down mouth to mouth by various people who sometimes had different versions of the truth. To me, Aunt Jane was Aunt Jane. I never even thought about who her father was or where her family came from. When you're very young you take those things for granted. So, it wasn't until I got older that these things became important to me. And even when I was in college I never thought much about it. These people I speak of were all still alive then. Aunt Jane was still there. She was an old lady, but she was still there. And it wasn't until after they were all

dead that I realized that I didn't know about them and their family background and then it was too late to get any firsthand information from that generation. But I did pick up quite a bit from conversations and I remember Aunt Jane telling us stories about her life and her family.

The Magee family lived up around Fallbrook, in back of Palomar Mountain, when your great-grandfather first came to the Santa Margarita. The Magees helped him protect his cattle from people who were stealing them from the Fallbrook side of the ranch and so the Magees became very close friends. People in those days in those sparsely settled areas became closer friends than they do nowadays. You don't pay too much attention to your neighbor now, but back then you did. So, they became extremely good friends of the family, and by the time I came along Aunt Jane had come to the Santa Margarita and was raising her beans on the Las Flores Mesa and had been for a good many years.

Aunt Jane's grandfather, on her mother's side, was Spanish. During the Napoleonic Wars he had been a Spanish diplomat in England until England and Spain became enemies and then all the Spanish were expelled. He moved to Peru and then to the Orient and finally he came to California. His name was Miguel Pedrorena and he had six daughters. One of them married Antonio Estudillo who built what they call "Ramona's Marriage Place" down in San Diego. Her Magee grandfather was a lieutenant in the United States Army who came out to California during the Mexican War and eventually was stationed at the Presidio in San Diego. He fell in love with one of the Estudillo girls and married her and sired quite a big family—and this was the Magees. So they were half Irish and half Spanish and they never did have a great deal of money, but they were people of great importance in the community around San Diego. The streets down there are all named after these early Spanish families. By comparison, the O'Neills were latecomers. Eighteen eighty-two was a pretty long time ago, but in California history, the O'Neills were just the Yankees who came in and took over from the original Spanish families. So we were actually not early Californians. We came here in '49 and got into the ranching business in San Diego County in 1882. But, meanwhile, the Altamiranos and the Estudillos and the Bandinis had been here since the Year One.

By the time your great-grandfather came to the Santa Margarita, the Magees had moved up to the Fallbrook area on the outskirts of the ranch. Like most Spanish and Irish families, the Magee family was very numerous. There was Victor Magee, Antonia Magee, and Billy and Louie and Jane and Anna and maybe some I can't remember. Shortly after my grandfather bought the Santa Margarita, Aunt Jane came down and took

over the Las Flores area to farm it, even though she was a woman. And
she had a brother, Hugh Magee—that was another one of them—her
older brother came down to manage it for her. She rented the land from
my grandfather and moved into the two-story Las Flores adobe that the
Forsters had built. And she raised beans and eventually became the
"Bean Queen" of Southern California. She grew beans on all those mesas
around the Las Flores, and although one of her brothers always supervised the workers, she was the brains of the outfit. It was a family farm
and the Magees were considered part of our family, too. And so when we
were kids we had Magee's coming out of our ears. They were all aunts
and uncles to us. On holidays like Christmas and Easter, they would all
come over to be with us at the ranch house.

Aunt Jane was a very astute business woman with her beans, but she
never married. She loved children and was very kind to us. With all the
Magee aunts' offspring and all the Baumgartner girls and boys, she had
more children staying with her at the Las Flores. There were always kids
around. The Las Flores was a haven for children and my brother, John,
and I would go over and stay with Aunt Jane for two or three weeks at
a time during the summers. We'd be under Aunt Jane's care and I don't
think we got away with a lot there, but we got away with more than we
could in our own family. And another advantage to staying at the Las
Flores: the Santa Margarita ranch house was eight or ten miles from the
beach but the Las Flores was only about a mile from the beach. During
the summer Aunt Jane and Auntie Wee and any other women staying at
the Las Flores would put all the kids in the buckboard and take us all to
the beach. Looking back on it, it was kind of a careless thing for them to
do with little kids. I was probably three or four years old and most of the
other children weren't much older and none of us could swim. And none
of the ladies could either! We'd paddle around in the surf or in the tidal
pool of Las Flores Creek while these women sat up on the sand and
talked and gossiped under their parasols. There wasn't a soul for twenty
miles in either direction; we were completely alone. But Aunt Jane had
these two dogs at the Las Flores, Bounce and Beauty. They were great big
St. Bernards and they had been raised with children and loved them. In

Las Flores Pond   Auntie Wee

those days we wore very voluminous swimming suits, because the human body wasn't to be overly exposed. So, while the women were up on the sand talking, Beauty would be the lifeguard. I'd go paddling around in the surf, and if I got out too far Beauty would come down into the water and grab the back of my suit and pull me back toward shore. She'd back up like a horse and pull me out and then go up and sit on the sand and watch us again. So summer at the Las Flores was a wonderful time for us kids. Aunt Jane would take care of us and take us down to the beach in the buckboard and we'd go swimming and have barbeques out on the lawn of the Las Flores ranch house. We had great faith that Aunt Jane could do anything.

Aunt Jane had an adobe house at the Las Flores. It was a Monterey-style adobe, very unusual for Southern California. It was two stories with a porch running along the second story across the front of the house. This porch faced the ocean but you couldn't actually see the water, because it was about a mile away. There were two great eucalyptus trees right in front of the porch and on hot summer days, Bounce and Beauty used to lie in their shade to get out of the heat. When they died, Aunt Jane told us that they'd be happier in the shade of those big gum trees, so they were buried there. Their wooden crosses are gone now, but they're still there.

When we stayed with Aunt Jane, we always slept in her bedroom which was upstairs on the second story. You went upstairs on the outside of the house. In those Spanish houses, there were never stairs on the inside; you'd have to go upstairs along an exterior wall. You know, when you're small, rooms look bigger than they actually are. When you go back to them after you're grown, they shrink quite a bit, but her room really was a big room. It took up the whole end of the house and in those days, we were very apt to sleep all in one room and all the kids bunked with Aunt Jane. She had a big double bed, one on those large Victorian beds, and Uncle John and I, when we were small kids, would all sleep with Aunt Jane, the three of us in the same bed.

And that room was the site of another great occasion, a weekly ritual. People took baths only once a week in those days. Before indoor plumbing and water heaters, a bath was a hard thing to get. They had a tank with a windmill, but the only running water was in the kitchen and it was cold water. So, they'd have to heat water on the stove in big pans. At the Las Flores—I don't know why it was done, because there were bedrooms downstairs—but Aunt Jane would heat the water on the stove down in the kitchen and lug these great big pails of hot water up the stairs to her bedroom. Then she'd pour it into one of those galvanized sheet metal tubs. They use to be quite common, but I don't think I've seen one in years. Then she'd take our clothes off—this would always be on Saturday—and the big flea catching scene would begin.

People don't understand this any more, but it's rather obvious: this was true of all ranches; it wasn't just the Santa Margarita or the Las Flores. Nowadays there's no livestock on ranches; it's all machines unless somebody wants to have a horse. But back then there were no machines and all the work was done by horses. So the barn was filled with horses, all different types of horses: dray horses to pull the buckboard or the wagons, heavier dray horses to pull the farm equipment, regular saddle horses, cutting horses, roping horses—a lot of horses. For convenience, the barn was only a hundred feet or so from the house. And there were pigpens and a chicken coop too. And all these animals had fleas. People in those days didn't know how to handle that kind of vermin, and they didn't care. A flea was a flea and so what? As kids we'd play around the barnyard and naturally we'd get a lot of fleas. I don't think the women of the house had as many as we did because they weren't around the livestock as much as we were. John and I used to go out into the pigpens and rope the pigs. We'd see the vaqueros roping cattle and we'd pretend we were vaqueros and rope pigs. So, we'd pick up a lot of fleas, and on Saturday nights we'd have our weekly bath. If we were at the Las Flores, Aunt Jane would dunk us in this hot water and scrub our backs and then she'd have to lug all that water downstairs again and throw it out off the porch. Meanwhile, throughout the bath, Aunt Jane would catch fleas and snap them between her thumb nails and she'd drop the dead ones into a pail of water. She'd get some off of us and then she'd start with our clothes until she couldn't find any more. This was all considered part of the normal weekly bath.

In the evening Aunt Jane would read us stories. One story that we particularly liked was a story about a hunter in Germany. We would always try to get her to read that particular story. It was a simple story about a hunter who was out in the forest hunting wolf when a terrible thunder storm started. He found a place under some rocks and brush out of the storm, a kind of nest. He crawled into this nest to get out of the wind and rain and he lay down and fell asleep. And a wolf had been caught by the storm too, and he crawled into this same place and lay down right next to the hunter and they slept together all night. In the morning, they both woke up and looked at each other and they got up and went their separate ways. That was all there was to the story. Looking back on it, it wasn't much of a story, but it was our favorite and every night we'd say, 'Aunt Jane, read us the story of the man and the wolf.' And years later, when I was a grown man, I went to see her. It was the last time I ever saw her and I asked her, 'Aunt Jane, where's the book with the story of the man and the wolf?' She said she didn't know and she looked for it but she couldn't find it. It was lost.

Sometimes young people remember very clearly in such detail as if it all happened yesterday. Sometimes events leave a clear impression on your mind because they are different. This particular episode was not unusual except for one facet: it happened at night and not in the daytime. Before 1911, transportation on the Santa Margarita was horse and wagon. We didn't go to church very often because it was eight miles to San Luis Rey. But we did go on Easter and maybe two or three other times during the year. And we did drive to Las Flores quite often even though it was about eight miles away. It was quite a road from the ranch house to Las Flores and I guess the drive would take a couple of hours, maybe two and a half hours. You had to climb out of the Santa Margarita canyon, go down a long canyon and up to what we called Cape Horn. From there on a clear day you could look for miles. There were canyons that ran through those mesas to the ocean, but they were all below and you looked right over them so you wouldn't even know they were there. The Las Flores house was down in Las Flores Canyon but you couldn't see that either. And beyond that were Aunt Jane's bean fields and Don Station. Her mesas were ideal places for beans because the fog would come in there and the beans liked that cool fog. Don Station was a big warehouse on the railroad siding where Aunt Jane's beans were stored awaiting shipment to market. When the Santa Fe built the station there, they wanted to call it 'Jerome Station' after my uncle, but the railroad already had a station in Arizona by that name. So, they called it 'Don Station' after the Spanish title of respect used in old California particularly for the owner of a rancho.

After they were threshed, the beans would be put into bags and stored at Don Station until the market price was right. Sometimes Aunt Jane's whole crop would be stored in the warehouse, her entire year's income. She used to tell John and me that she was going to get us a wishing stick. She meant a wishing wand, but she always called it a wishing stick. And she'd say, 'When I give you your wishing stick, your first wish must be for the bean crop to be good this year.' That was the most important thing we could do for her.

These womenfolk in the Magee family were all ranch people and Aunt Jane was a wonderful horsewoman. She could ride a horse, but by the time I came along I suppose she was in her forties and she didn't ride horses anymore, but drove her wagon. She had a two-horse team with a buckboard, and when we'd go to the Las Flores she'd come over to the Santa Margarita in the morning and have lunch with us and invite us to go back with her. John and I and maybe my other brother, Richard, would run to our rooms and pack our little valise. It was a little black leather bag and it belonged to my grandfather, but when we got to stay with Aunt Jane it was our overnight bag. Then we'd jump into the buckboard with Aunt Jane and off we'd go.

The one trip to the Las Flores that I remember distinctly was in 1908. It was Aunt Jane, John and I in the buckboard with two horses. Nobody else. Aunt Jane sitting there with a veil over her head and the reins in her hands. For some reason we had gotten a late start and by the time we got up Cape Horn it was dark. Aunt Jane was driving us children up this steep road at night. It wasn't dangerous, but most women today, and most men for that matter, wouldn't attempt it. Even though in those days when women were considered to be much more frail and weak than they are today, nobody thought anything about a woman taking children eight miles in a buckboard over ranch roads in the dark. And as we came to the top of the Cape Horn Canyon—and that was the place you could look way down the coast—we could see a fire burning off in the distance. Because it was dark we couldn't tell how far away it was, but it was at least a couple of miles. Aunt Jane said, 'My God, the warehouse is on fire! Jeromie, the warehouse is burning and all my beans are going up. You take the reins,' and she gave me the reins and got off the buckboard. Sometimes she used to give us kids the reins and let us drive the team, but she was always sitting right next to us. But this time she was so upset that she got off and left me alone. There really wasn't any danger. The horses knew the road and just kept tromping along and so I didn't really have to steer them. But here I was, five years old, holding the reins. It was pitch black and this fire was burning two or three miles up ahead. It was so dramatic to me as a little kid that I'm sure that's why I remember it so well. My brother John was asleep in the back of the buckboard. John was famous for falling asleep every time he sat down. Aunt Jane walked in back of the wagon, saying the rosary with her beads in her hands and we moved along like that for a half hour or so. Why she didn't walk in front of the wagon or say her rosary in the wagon, I don't know. A little closer to God, I guess. But she walked behind the buckboard for two or three miles and we'd go down into these dips and when we came up, the fire would be closer yet. We finally arrived at the Las Flores house and Billy and Louie Magee were there. They used to thresh the beans at night a lot, because the beans would be damp and easier to thresh. When they were through threshing, they'd have all this bean straw which wasn't any good for cattle feed or anything, so they would burn it. And Billy and Louie had forgotten to tell her that they were going to burn bean straw up on the mesa that night. Her bean crop was safe. Aunt Jane was very religious in a Spanish-Catholic, Irish-Catholic way. Religion played a part in her daily life, more so than it would in most people's. She was very devout and things religious weren't far from her mind at all times. So, when adversity struck, Aunt Jane's answer was to get off the wagon and walk behind it in the dark, saying her beads.

Aunt Jane had a sister, Luisa. We called her Auntie Wee but she wasn't a full sister to Aunt Jane. She was an illegitimate child of one of the Magee uncles and an Indian girl. This uncle had a buckboard and drove all over Southern California and everywhere was his home. So, there were Magees all over the place. Aunt Jane's mother from the Estudillo

Auntie Wee
ca. 1925

side of the family took the girl and raised her when her Indian mother died. Auntie Wee was about the same age as Uncle Jerome who was born in 1861. By the time I came along, they both were very much in middle age. She was half Indian and looked it. She was built a little bit like Babe Ruth. She was big chested, but not overly so, and she had small legs and very small ankles. She was a fine looking woman without being beautiful and she was a fixture around the ranch house. She took care of your great-grandfather when he got to the point where he needed nursing and then she took care of your great-grandmother until she died. After that she was the housekeeper at the ranch house until she retired, many years after I went away to college. In other words, she was a perpetual housekeeper and nurse but not treated as such but as a member of the family. She took care of us kids much of the time and she was very kind to us. She was strict, but very kind. She was very proud and could be very firm on some things. If Auntie Wee said, 'This is the way it is going to be,' that's the way it was, as far as we kids were concerned. She could tell Uncle Jerome off pretty well, too, but never in front of us.

On our honeymoon Doris and I went down to the ranch, among other places. Auntie Wee had retired by that time and was living in Oceanside in a little cottage not far from the beach. We were going to call on her there and take her up to visit the Magees at Las Flores. Aunt Jane was still alive then, living at the Las Flores where she'd always lived and she had invited us up for lunch. Las Flores is eight or ten miles up the highway from Oceanside, and after we drove across the Santa Margarita River and up to the top of those mesas we came to an immigration stop. For years there has always been an immigration checkpoint up on those mesas where they stop cars looking for Mexicans without papers. So, they flagged down the car and a young border patrol officer came up to the window and asked my name and citizenship. I told him that I was Jerome Baumgartner and that that was my wife in the back seat. Auntie Wee was sitting next to me in the front seat and he looked over at her Indian brown face. But before he could say anything, Auntie Wee sat up straight and rigid and looked him right in the eye and said, 'Young man, I was here on this ranch before you were born.' This nice young officer just smiled at her and said, 'Yes, ma'am.' and waved us on. Auntie Wee could have that effect on you if she felt definite about something.

Today, people can see more events than when I was a child. In those days you could read about great happenings in the newpaper and that's as close as they ever got. But through television, people are used to seeing great events and sporting events and political events even while they are taking place. We've gotten so spoiled that we take these things we see pretty much for granted. I remember a few years ago we had a few people over to the house to watch an important football game. The game was played in Miami and we kept switching over to another game played in Chicago, and at half time they showed one of the astronauts walking on the moon. We all watched these events taking place in two different cities and even on the moon and everybody looked at them with the casualness of people looking out their windows at the traffic going by. When I was very young, people never got to see these things, and if they did it was such an exciting experience that they never forgot.

I remember that in 1908 I saw the Great White Fleet. Theodore Roosevelt had concocted the idea of this fleet as a way of showing the world and the American people that the United States had become a world power. So he had the ships of this fleet painted all white instead of the usual grey and the fleet sailed around the world for everyone to see. The Great White Fleet got a lot of publicity and the newspapers followed its cruise daily. Every day there would be an article on some aspect of the Great White Fleet. Eventually it sailed into San Diego and it stayed in port there for several days. San Diego was a long way to go in those days and so naturally no one from the ranch went all the way to San Diego just to see the Great White Fleet. Only people living in San Diego or close by had that opportunity. But when it left San Diego, it was to sail up the coast to Los Angeles and then San Francisco and the newspapers printed its schedule so everyone along the Southern California coast would know when it was going to pass by and could go out to see it.

Everyone in our family had followed this cruise and so we all wanted to see it sail by the ranch. This was a big event and big events were unusual in our lives. So, the day before it was due to pass the ranch, the whole family headed for the Las Flores ranch house so we could spend the night there and drive out to the Las Flores bluffs the next morning. Everyone had an overnight bag and we drove over in the surrey and the buckboard and Aunt Jane made a big dinner for this hoard of house guests. I think that night she had more guests than she had ever had. It was like a holiday, but it wasn't like the Fourth of July or Christmas because this didn't happen every year and no one knew what to expect. We all got up the next morning and the women packed lunch in baskets and everyone drove over to the bluffs in wagons and buckboards. At that time of year the Las Flores bluffs are covered with wild mustard, but the women found a patch of open ground near the edge and spread out tablecloths. We had a very fancy lunch in honor of this great event. The fleet was scheduled to sail by the bluffs about one o'clock in the afternoon, so we made sure to be through our meal and have everything put back in the wagons by then.

It was a clear, warm day that made the ocean bluer than the sky and everybody sat on the top of the bluffs talking, the women in the shade of their parasols. In those days, women were supposed to have very white complexions, so they always carried parasols if they were to be outdoors. Suntans were not at all popular and no self-respecting woman would have one. It seemed to me that we waited quite a long time, talking and keeping an eye on the horizon down the coast. Everyone, including the adults, wanted to be the one to announce the arrival of the Great White Fleet. Finally, we saw the smoke from the ships' stacks and everyone jumped up, as if being five feet taller would allow them to look over the horizon at the ships themselves. But it seemed to take so long before those puffs of smoke had the little white dots at their bases that we'd come to see.

Slowly the ships sailed up the coast toward us, and as they did they grew bigger and with every minute that went by some new detail would come into view and this picture we'd come to see was brought more and more into focus. The purpose of this cruise was to be seen by as many people as possible, so the ships hugged the coastline as closely as they safely could. Even when it was some way off, we could hear the BOOM, BOOM of the ships cannons as they fired a salute to those who had come to watch this parade. And the booms got louder as the ships came closer, until they were nearly up to our bluff. Then we heard the music. The navy band was on the deck of the lead ship playing military music, and when this ship came right abreast of us we could hear the music as clearly as if the band were in the bandstand on a Sunday in the park. I distinctly remember that when they got up to us they were playing *Stars and Stripes Forever,* and I could even hear the flute part. And each ship went by slowly and proudly, and we could see the sailors on deck in their white uniforms waving their caps at us. And all of us, Uncle Jerome and Aunt Jane and Uncle Dick, our whole family waved back. But nobody said a word. It was one of those moments when you want to take in everything: the music and the white ships against the blue ocean with the white uniforms of the sailors and the smell of the ocean breeze and the wild mustard. I was only five years old at the time and it's a scene I'll never forget. Today, I'd see it on T.V. and it'd probably not mean much more to me than a beer commercial. Today, that scene probably wouldn't be noteworthy enough even to put on television, but it was one of the most stirring things I've ever seen. In some ways, television is not an improvement. We see more, but we miss more, too, and we don't even know it.

CHAPTER

The Baumgartner Family

S YD MADE a wonderful dinner—roast beef and Yorkshire pudding—my father's favorite. Everyone enjoyed the meal, so the dinner table conversation was only brief phrases between bites and swallows. After dinner we moved back into our seats in front of the fire and my father was ready to begin again. I started the tape recorder.

I was born in Oakland, but when I was three months old I was brought down to the Santa Margarita to join my sister and brothers on the ranch. My mother brought me down on the train. The train service of that time, 1903, wasn't much different from the way it is now. The trip from San Francisco to Los Angeles took nearly all day and then it was about three hours to Oceanside. The ranch house was on the ranch line and not on the mainline, but the Las Flores house was about a mile from the Las Flores Station on the mainline. We used to call it 'the Tank' because it had a water tank near the corrals where we shipped cattle. There was no other way to travel in those days, so a lot of the trains stopped at those small stations. My mother brought me down to the ranch by herself, quite a trip for a woman in those days. She got off the train at the Tank, the Las Flores Station. It was dark by that time, but the people at the

107

ranch were expecting her. She was met by Aunt Jane and Auntie Wee and they greeted her and admired the new baby for a few minutes and then got into Aunt Jane's carriage and drove over to the Las Flores ranch house. We stayed there overnight and the next day we drove over to the main ranch house. There's nothing particularly important about this story except that was the first night I spent on the ranch and the reason I can tell you about it is that I was reminded of it many times during my childhood. Auntie Wee never stopped telling me about that night. She'd say, 'Jeromie, your mother was so tired that we put her right to bed so she could get a good sleep. You didn't stop crying the whole night. You probably don't remember that night at the Las Flores, but I walked that porch all night long with you. You owe me something for that.' She never forgot to remind me that I had kept her awake all night. Apparently I wasn't too happy about being on the ranch, but, believe me, that was the last time I felt that way.

My brothers and my sister and I—and in a certain sense particularly I myself—were thrown into a ranch life that was pretty special. I was six years old before I ever got off the ranch except to go to Oceanside once in a while. We had a wonderful time. It was not the kind of a life that most people were living, but we were oblivious to that. We didn't know there was any other kind of life to live. You must remember this: there are thousands of boys who have been raised on farms and ranches all over America. They were not people of great means and they got up in the morning and had cows to milk and work to do. They were hard-working, and in that way they had much more of a ranch life than I. In that sense, we had it just the other way around. We had a very large ranch house and all the help that was required to make it run well. So, we had a very easy time when it came to ranch life. But, on the other hand, it was in an area and at a time that ranch life was still attuned to early California traditions. A great many of the people who worked on the ranch were not from Mexico but were from Capistrano and San Luis Rey, and their families had come with the padres in the old days. They were fourth-generation families. In my day on the Santa Margarita, places like Capistrano were made up of people of Spanish decent. That was the difference between our situation and that of people living in the Midwest and other rural areas. Our way of life had begun way back in the Spanish and Mexican days and was pretty much the same as it had always been. We were raised in a magnificent ranch house with 19th century accommodations, with no electricity or indoor plumbing. But what I have to say about daily life could be said about life anywhere in rural America of that time. The good thing about it was, from my point of view, that it was different from any other time because the ranch was going through a change from the horse and buggy days to the mechanized modern days. Transportation hadn't really changed for hundreds of years. The first car I ever saw came to the Santa Margarita about 1909. It was a White Steamer and I was six years old. The ranch didn't get its own car for several years after that. In other words, during my early years on the ranch, we could travel about as fast as Columbus had four hundred years earlier.

The people on the ranch who took care of us were ranchers and they were very busy people. It was very important that the home be operated smoothly, and from the time I arrived at the ranch my Aunt Alice was the one making sure the ranch house ran properly. She lived there until after my grandfather died in 1910. She was our closest female relative and she took the place of our mother. And Auntie Wee was there, too, taking care of my grandfather and sometimes us kids as well. My parents were living in San Francisco and we children lived way down on the ranch in Southern California. Why that was I don't know. It may have been because of my brother Richard's health. It wasn't for lack of room at the family home on 17th Street. God, that big house could have housed ten kids. My mother and father would come down to visit us at Christmas time and in the summer, mostly my mother, because my father couldn't leave his work. He was always there at Christmas. But we saw more of Uncle Jerome than we did my father. We were very well cared for, but those people never let us forget our mother—never. During all that time, we'd get postcards from my mother and my father. We couldn't read, so they'd read them to us. They were very loyal in that way. They didn't try to usurp any prerogatives that didn't belong to them. And yet, they acted very much like our parents. But when the time came, we went up to San Francisco to school. My sister, Bessie, was six years older than I, so, by the time I can remember, she had left the ranch to go to school in the City. I never knew Bessie on the ranch. My brother, Richard, was four years older than I, and he'd come down to the ranch during the Christmas and summer vacations, but then he'd disappear again when school began. So, it was John and I on the ranch together until 1909 when he left for school. And then there were no children at the ranch house but me, and I left to go up to school in 1911. I had no companionship with children my own age except when I went to stay with Aunt Jane at the Las Flores where some of her nieces might be visiting. So, the two years that I spent by myself were very pleasant years, but they were different. I didn't miss children. I had no way of knowing what life with them was like. But I don't think I ever got over it. When I came up to school I was very nervous. All of a sudden I was put into a class with a teacher and all those kids, and I didn't feel at ease. There was a shyness that crept into me then that I've never quite gotten over.

I made a great mistake early in my life. My parents weren't particularly useful in helping me avoid it. I'm not blaming them for it. There's nothing to blame anyone for. My father pretty much let my mother run the show as far as us kids were concerned. My father was a Lutheran and my mother was Catholic. He wasn't a strict Lutheran, but he certainly wasn't a Catholic. And my mother was a strict Irish Catholic. It was understood between my father and mother that we would be raised Catholic, but we were not sent to Catholic schools. I never went to a Catholic school in my life and neither did any of my brothers. I went to Grant School for grammar school and then Lowell High School like everyone in the neighborhood. My brother John went to those schools, too, and so did Richard, in his own way. But they didn't send me right to school when I came up from the ranch. Although I was six years old when I left the ranch, I didn't start school until I was seven. So all during grammar school, I was a year behind the other kids. That didn't mean a thing until I got to high school. But when I got to high school, I began to notice that my classmates were younger than I was and I thought I wanted to go through high school in three years and catch up. It was a stupid idea and I'm sorry my mother didn't try to stop me. But she didn't know much about education, so she didn't argue about it. So, I was at Lowell for only a year and then I went to a private school called Bates. It was accredited by the University of California and Stanford and it was a very small school. I went through high school in three years which was the greatest mistake of my educational life. When I got to Cal, I really wasn't mature enough for college and I never was a very good student anyway. So I wound up flunking out after the first six months—a shattering experience for me.

I never took to the ranching business very well. Oh, I liked riding horses and staying in the vaquero camps and sleeping out because it was exciting and romantic to me. As I grew up I remember thinking that the things we did on the ranch were fun, but looked at them as a side issue for me. I never really entertained the idea of centering my life around that sort of career. My brother John, on the other hand, really took to it from the time he was very small. John was very lucky in that way. You seldom meet someone who knows what they want to do for a lifelong career so young, but John did. Before he went to grammar school I think John had it in his head that this ranching life was what he was going to do and he never deviated from that. He went through elementary and high school with the aim of going to the University of California at Davis and studying to be a cattleman. He was smart enough to realize that the whole business was changing. His grandfather and Uncle Jerome had learned the business purely through their experience on the Chowchilla and Santa Margarita ranches. But your Uncle John was the first generation to go to agricultural school and learn the business from the scientific point of view. So he's very progressive. He remembers the old days and they're very much in his mind, but he realizes that the old ways aren't necessarily the best. When he went to college, Davis was a cow college; all that was taught there was ranching and growing crops, an agricultural college in the true sense of the term. It's grown to be a big university now, but when John went there there were probably no more than a thousand students. The only people who went there were the sons of farmers and ranchers. He graduated about 1926 and went down to the Santa Margarita to work for a while under Charlie Hardy who had become manager after Uncle Jerome died. The old timers on the ranch didn't think much of college boys, kind of looked down on these college kids who knew all the answers. So, Charlie Hardy told John that he thought it was fine for John to work on the Santa Margarita, but why didn't he go out and get a ranch of his own and learn the business in a smaller way. So, John got a ranch on the top of those mountains between Salinas and Hollister, near Fremont Peak. I think my parents helped him buy it. He ran cattle up there by himself for two or three years. He learned the business the hard way, which was probably a good thing. But he finally went broke. The price of beef dropped and it cost him more to run his operation than he got back on the sale of his cattle. So, he went to work for the state agricultural commission and when things got better he leased more land and he's been in the cattle business ever since. But, then, when they split up the ranch the Floods took the lower half and we took the middle and the O'Neill's took the upper part. So, we no longer had a partnership with the Floods. The Baumgartners owned the San Onofre and the San Mateo, and the Floods owned the southern part of the ranch. Uncle John went down to run our part. We called the ranch the San Onofre and John had a new brand made up for it. The Floods kept the TO brand from the Santa Margarita.

The fire had burned down to red and orange embers and I asked my father to stop for a moment while I went out for another log. Syd went into the kitchen, so, by the time I came back, my dad was alone in the room, rocking slowly back and forth in the wicker rocker and staring into the fire, remembering.

My other brother Richard was four years older than I. Incidentally, he was entirely a different type from John or me. You've seen pictures of him and you've seen pictures of my grandfather, Richard O'Neill, and they're dead ringers for each other. He was a very popular man. Everybody liked him very much. He had a mind of his own and he was pretty smart, but school and he didn't get along well together. In those days schools, at least the schools in San Francisco, decided if a student should be promoted to the next grade. If he wasn't promoted, then he had to take the class over again. That's what they did in those days. I don't know what they do now. They tell me they don't leave anybody behind. But if you were on the borderline, they could put you on trial for the next class. So, every year when promotion time came around, they'd put Richard up on trial and he'd go on to the next grade. He spent his entire school life trying to get promoted. And he always got through by the skin of his teeth. He had a great personality and all the teachers loved him, so they always put him on trial rather than keep him back. And this happened at every promotion. He was never promoted, but was always put on trial. Then came the big moment when he was suppose to graduate from grammar school. Then they couldn't put him up for trial to get him into high school. He either graduated or he didn't. But he got to high school and I don't know if he ever got his grammar school diploma or not. Then he went to Lowell High School and he didn't do any better in high school than he had in grammer school. He never read a book in his life. He was a smart guy, but he would have nothing to do with book learning at all.

The family had a home built at 2910 Vallejo Street in San Francisco and we moved in there in 1916. My brother John and I shared a room and Richard had the room next to us, so we were very much aware of his nocturnal activities. I can't remember Richard having these problems as a younger child, but when he got to be a teenager he started walking in his sleep. He wouldn't do it every night, but often enough so that if you heard something going on in the middle of the night, you'd guess it was Richard and you'd probably be right. Sometimes he'd walk down the hall to my parents' room to tell them something. At one point, he tried to break himself of this sleepwalking by tying his bathrobe sash to his arm and tying the other end to his bed. That worked pretty well at first. When he got up in his sleep, the sash would yank his arm and he'd wake up. But he began to untie the sash in his sleep, and then he was walking all around the house in the middle of the night again. For a while he was having dreams that someone was trapped under his bed and would get up and take his bed apart to rescue him. John and I would be in the next room and we'd hear all this clanking from Richard's room and we'd get up and go into his room. There'd be Richard sitting on the floor taking his bedsprings apart. We'd wake him up and sometimes, if we hadn't caught him in time, he'd have practically his whole bed disassembled all over the floor and it would take him half the night to put it back together before he could go back to sleep. Once, he had another dream that he had to rescue someone and he jumped out his bedroom window. Our bedrooms were on the second story and Richard's room had two windows. Fortunately, he jumped out the window that was over the garage roof, because if he'd jumped out the other one he'd have fallen two stories. When he landed on the garage roof, he woke up. He hadn't hurt himself, but he was afraid to climb back in the window. Mr. Tynon lived down the street and he had his own patrolman at night, and Richard was worried that Tynon's patrolman would see him climbing into the window and shoot him, thinking he was a burglar. So, Richard climbed down the drainpipe to the street. There he was, standing on the sidewalk in his pajamas and barefeet at three o'clock in the morning. He walked around to the front door and rang the bell to get someone to let him in. Not surprisingly, the doorbell woke up everyone in the house and we all went downstairs to see who could be at the front door at that ungodly hour. I think my parents were afraid that it was news that someone had died or some other tragedy. John and I were excited by the mystery of the whole thing. We were all shocked to see Richard standing on the steps in his pajamas. At first, my parents were relieved that it was just Richard and that he was all right. But then my mother became upset when Richard told us what had happened. My father was annoyed. And John and I were in awe of Richard's adventure. Richard himself acted very nonchalant about the whole business and went up to bed. He outgrew his sleep-walking sometime in his twenties, but we had quite a few exciting nights before he did.

My brother Richard had something wrong with his legs. As I recall, as a young boy he was healthy. He was my big brother and he was four years older than I and he rode horses and did all the things a boy could do and I looked up to him. But when he got to be sixteen, he began to have troubles with his knees. Arthritis is what he had. But at that time they knew very little about it and they didn't have any effective treatment for it. It was just a matter of staving it off as long as possible. He was on crutches part of the time. He'd be well sometimes and sometimes not. By the time I went to college, it had gone up to his hips and he couldn't walk at all. But then, he'd have these times when he was fine, as if he was cured. He'd walk with a cane but I don't think he really needed it. He liked to be a snappy dresser and I think the cane was just part of the act. It was during one of these times when he appeared to be cured that he married Margaret Durbrow. He was working in a bond office in downtown San Francisco and he got married and they had an apartment of their own and everything was fine. But then it flared up again and he began to have terrible trouble with his hips and they finally operated on him. He had one of the finest doctors in the country, but the operation was very unusual for that time. The doctor carved him a new set of hips and it shortened his height about two inches. He wasn't very tall to start with but then he was very much shorter. He never walked without crutches after the operation. He and Margaret had to move into the family home because he needed constant nursing care. So, he and Margaret had a married life all tangled up with the in-laws, which was not always the happiest situation, but everybody tried to make the best of it. They were not able to establish a real home of their own and he was never to go back to work again. They were married about twelve years and eventually all this trouble and pain built up to a brain hemmorhage and he died in 1940. But he was a great guy. He was by far the most popular guy in the Baumgartner family.

Richard and my father didn't see eye to eye about anything. My father was a rather shy man. He was not easily approachable and not at all jolly and particularly not when it came to politics. He was a kind man, but he had a way of exaggerating when he was discussing politics. The whole family would be sitting at the dinner table and my father would get all worked up about something political and he'd hammer on the table and carry on. We'd sit at the table and let Pa talk because the rest of us didn't want to get into a fight. But my brother Richard couldn't keep his mouth shut and he would catch Pa in one of his exaggerations and my father didn't like to be made wrong. Nobody does, but he wasn't much of a diplomat about it. Richard would call him on something he'd said and they'd go 'round and 'round about it. My brother would usually be right, but my father couldn't stand being contradicted. Then my mother would get mad as hell at the two of them. This didn't happen at every meal, but often enough to keep everyone on edge.

Some of these dinner table unpleasantries started long before I can remember. When I was an infant on the ranch it was the Victorian age and my grandfather was head of the household, and in the Victorian age that meant that he was practically king. In the evenings the whole family would sit down to dinner and it was kind of a ritual, very formal for an everyday event. My grandfather always sat at the head of the table, at the place of honor and presided over everything. Actually he didn't do anything; the women would be up and scurrying around with plates and bowls from the kitchen to the table. But his big moment would come when it was time to carve the roast. Very often we would have a roast for dinner and my grandfather, having been a butcher, took great pride in demonstrating to the whole family his ability to carve a roast correctly. He always made a big show of the carving, even though everybody had been convinced for years that he could really carve a roast or a turkey or whatever we were having. But he always went through the carving with great showmanship, as if there were still doubters at his table. And when my mother married my father, she expected my father to carve the turkey or roast as well as my grandfather had. To her it was a test of manhood, I think. And, of course, my father failed the test time and again. I think he thought that carving shouldn't take on the importance that it did for my mother, but he couldn't resist rising to the challenge every time. He would sit up straight in his chair with the turkey on the big platter in front of him and the carving knife and fork in his hands and he'd study that bird like he was looking at a map. Then he would start, at first very deliberately and my mother would sit down at the other end of the table watching him and quietly coach him by shaking her head when she thought he was doing it wrong and mutter audibly under her breath. Meanwhile, my father would be quietly swearing at the bird and his hand would move the knife in a more frenzied manner until the whole table would be shaking and the wine glasses swaying. And it always happened that when he came to a joint and he couldn't cut through it, his swearing would get quite loud but not so loud that you couldn't heard my mother muttering at the other end of the table. I used to hate the part of Christmas dinner when my father carved the Christmas turkey. It was never pleasant during normal times when just us kids were present, but the whole show took on even larger proportions in front of guests.

That never happened at my grandfather's table. Everyone, including my mother, would watch with awe while he dissected the roast or turkey or whatever was for dinner. And all the children ate at the table. That was part of the ritual. This was a family table and everyone in the family was to eat at the table. So, when I was very young and I mean one or two years old, Aunt Alice or Auntie Wee would bring me to the table and hold me in their laps during the meal. And apparently sometimes I would cry like babies often do and I'd be crying and screaming and disrupting the whole meal until my grandfather would ask angrily, 'What the hell does that child want? Whatever it is, give it to him, God damn it!' My grandfather believed in certain theories about childrearing, but not at the dinner table. He was the king, and if I made enough noise anything I wanted was mine.

My father loved to travel. It was in his blood. He had never been to Europe, which wasn't at all unusual for those days, because it took two weeks just to get to New York. So most Americans didn't go to Europe their entire lives. He always wanted to go, but for my mother travelling was something she could do without. My father had been trying for years to get her to go with him to Europe and the last hurdle my father had to get her over was her fear of the boat trip. Finally, in 1912 she agreed reluctantly to go. They had their trunks all packed and their tickets were bought and they were all set to go when the *Titanic* sank. That was the end of that trip. Pa could have shot the captain of the *Titanic*. My mother never did quite get over the sinking of the *Titanic,* but they finally did get to Europe in 1925. I was a junior in college then. My brother Richard went with them. He was up and around at that time, but he was walking with a cane. They were gone three or four months and my father did a lot of his painting there.

When my father was painting stage scenes and railroad car interiors back in Milwaukee, he developed a lot of technique, and he later took up painting as a hobby. He was pretty good and he used to like to paint landscapes and seascapes down at the Santa Margarita. He never had any formal training in art. He taught himself and he learned by experimenting. He was rather shy about his art and we didn't have enough knowledge about it to discuss it with him intelligently. I think he was a reactionary when it came to his ideas about art. I think he liked the Impressionists like Monet and Renoir, but he considered much of the art of the 1910s and '20s to be grotesque. He founded a group called The Society for Sanity in Art and he and his artist friends actively opposed the works of progressive artists they didn't understand. Modern art was another subject he and Richard used to battle over at the dinner table.

After I was born, my parents moved from Oakland over to the O'Neill home on 17th Street in San Francisco. By that time, all the O'Neills were living down on the ranch, so the 17th Street house became my parents' permanent home. I think they moved there because my father had an office in San Francisco. He was an architectural delineator. That was his term for it. He was not an architect. He had no license because he'd only finished grammar school back in Milwaukee. But he had studied architecture on his own at the library, and architects would bring him the blueprints of a house or building. He would take the plans and translate them into a picture of what the building was going to look like when it was completed. It was a very specialized business and took a great deal of talent. When I was a kid, he had his office in the Humboldt Bank Building on Market Street, furnished with big drafting tables and T-squares. He did a great deal of business, but it was not the sort of business you'd make a fortune at, but he made a living. My father was a very talented man, but he was not a financial success.

Every family has its peculiarities, and if it's your family you don't notice them because you've grown up with them and you're used to them. But, when you get married and bring your bride into your family, then these eccentricities that you've never particularly noticed become troublesome. When two people become engaged and your families have nothing in common—they don't even come from the same town and have never met each other—you have to have a formal meeting when the two families get introduced to each other. They all look at each other like a bunch of stray dogs. There's nothing more critical than a couple of mothers looking at who is marrying their children. Fathers aren't usually so bad. So, when your mother and I got engaged, we had this meeting of the clans and it was murder.

To be honest about it, I think my mother had pictured me marrying one of her friends' daughters. She knew a lot of people and they all seemed to have daughters. I knew them all, but somehow they didn't appeal to me. So, I think that when I became engaged to Doris my mother was not too happy from the start. My father was fine, strange as it may seem. He had met Doris. She had come to dinner at our house. She was a very attractive girl and my father wasn't blind. But my mother was much more critical. She wanted to know what kind of family Doris came from, so we had the Forestiers to dinner. I was working at the Mark Hopkins Hotel at the time and I didn't get off work until about 5:30. Doris had finished her modelling work at Livingston Brothers earlier, so she was there when I arrived home. I went up to shower and shave and the preliminary fireworks began even before I got back downstairs.

My brother Richard and his wife Margaret were downstairs with your mother and they had all the sympathy in the world for this situation. They helped calm Doris' nerves. The doorbell rang and my mother answered the door and it was Mr. and Mrs. Forestier and Doris' brother, Ed. Ed was no help during the evening either. He was about eighteen and didn't much like these fancy people from Pacific Heights. They walked in the door and my mother said, 'Good evening.' And your Grandma Forestier said, 'Good evening. Where's Jerry?' 'Jerome,' my mother corrected her. My mother never liked the name Jerry and she insisted on the name Jerome even though all my friends called me Jerry. So, Grandma Forestier started off the proceedings with a *faux pas* and my mother fired the first shot of the evening in response. In the front hall was a long table against the wall and on it was a statue my father had bought in Europe, and he was very proud of it. It was the bust of some woman, a reproduction of a famous Renaissance statue, I think. Doris' mother was wearing a big hat with a veil and she took it off and put it on my father's favorite statue as if it were a hat stand. God, she couldn't have done anything worse if she'd planned it. My mother and father thought they had a gem of interior decoration and this statue was its centerpiece. Poor Doris was very nervous to begin with, and by the way the evening had started she could see that things were not going to go smoothly at all.

I was downstairs by that time and we all went into the livingroom before dinner. My father had some of his paintings on the walls and they started talking about his art. That was fine. It gave everyone a subject of conversation. In those days, Mrs. Forestier was fairly young and a fine looking woman. She asked my father to take her up to his studio and show her his other paintings. It wasn't that 'take-me-upstairs-and-show-my-your-etchings' routine. She was just interested in my father's painting, but you could see that my mother didn't appreciate it at all.

My father and mother weren't drinkers. They had nothing against liquor; my father had been very much against Prohibition. He drank wine with his meals, but we didn't usually have cocktails. Once in a while my parents would serve drinks if someone of particular importance was coming to dinner. We didn't have cocktails that night. My mother served a very formal dinner and that was all right, but it didn't make anybody more relaxed. My father was okay and my mother was fine, too. But it was the meeting of the clans and such things don't always work out the way they should. Your mother was eventually so unnerved that she had to go upstairs and throw up in the bathroom.

His whole face smiled in amusement at the memory of that night. What a wonderful trait to be able to turn what must have been a torturous evening into a light-hearted memory filled with humor. I wondered if he learned this from Uncle Dick—certainly not from Uncle Jerome.

CHAPTER ELEVEN

The Vaquero Camps

THE VAQUERO CAMPS were always fun for John and me and we'd spend as much of our summers as we could living with the vaqueros. I think we were a nuisance to them, but they were very patient. We were the nephews of the Big Boss and they had to look out for us so we didn't get into trouble. Steve Peters kept an eye on me when we were riding to make sure I didn't ride into a dangerous situation.

The vaquero camps were always in the same place year after year. There were camps at San Onofre, San Mateo, Las Pulgas and the Mission Viejo. For some reason I remember the San Onofre camp best. It was up the canyon about a mile or so above the railroad tracks and we always called it 'the gum trees,' not San Onofre camp but the Gum Trees. When we camped there we always camped in the same place, beneath three huge eucalyptus trees down by the creek. When I was very young they were just plain camps and everybody had a blanket roll and slept on the ground. And when there was going to be a rodeo, the vaqueros would have to get up very early to go round up the cattle to drive them down to the rodeo grounds where the cattle buyer would select cattle for shipment to market. We'd get up in the dark and ride single file in the dark for maybe an hour. No one talked and it would be so cold that I couldn't feel the reins in my hands. Every so often we'd all stop and Steve Peters would say, 'Chulo, you go up this canyon,' and Chulo and another vaquero would disappear into the darkness. He'd send two men at a time up each canyon and we wouldn't see them again until late in the morning when they'd drive whatever cattle they'd found onto the rodeo ground. After all the men had gone off to do their assigned work, Steve and I would ride on alone. He'd always take me with him so he could look out for me. Steve always called me 'Chomie' with his Spanish accent. My brothers called me 'Jome,' Aunt Jane and Auntie Wee called me 'Jomie' but Steve called me 'Chomie.' And I can hear him say it yet, 'Chomie, you come with me.' When he said it, his voice didn't have the same authority in it as when he was giving orders to his men. It had some of the authority and I liked that, to be treated like one of the men. But some of the harshness was gone, and in its place you could hear some of the gentleness like when he spoke to my mother. And if I started to do anything that was dangerous, he'd say, 'Now, Chomie, you stay here and I'll do that.' Once in a while, he'd have to rope a steer to get it out of the brush and God! it was a picture to see that man rope. He would sit up straight in the saddle and no part of his body would move except the arm that was swinging the reata. He'd hold his head back with his chin and goatee in front of him and that reata would sail out straight as a wire and in no time at all he'd have that steer out of the brush.

In 1915, Uncle Jerome decided to get a little modern and had bunkhouses built where the vaqueros had always made camp. Actually, they were more like barracks than bunkhouses. They were just board and batten buildings with wood floors—hotter than hell in the summertime. You had to walk up a couple of stairs to enter them and you'd be in a long room with three-foot shelf-beds made of wood along each wall. Every six and a half feet there was a headboard about a foot high, and in between the headboards were the bunks. They were of very simple construction. You and I could build all of the bunks in a day. They were nothing more than wooden boards for the shelf and a narrow board nailed to the side to hold the hay in. The vaqueros would pile a little hay on the boards and spread their blankets out on that. It got cold in the wintertime, but it wasn't anything like Wyoming, no blizzards or snow. There weren't any stoves or fireplaces and besides, the camps weren't used much in the winter. But they were used frequently during the summers and they got hot as ovens. This was the way it was on all the ranches in those days. The ranch provided the workers with three meals a day and a place to sleep, period. The workers provided their own blankets. The ranch gave them three meals a day, seven days a week and paid them. The vaqueros got more money than the laborers. The average laborer got about $30 a month and the vaqueros got about $45, which wasn't bad as it sounds. It wasn't what you'd call princely pay, but $45 was a lot of money in those days.

In the bunkhouses you had to walk through the big sleeping room and go through the door at the end to get to another room which was the kitchen/diningroom, all in one. There was an old woodburning range and a long table with benches for the men to use while eating their meals. There was no running water, but there was always a creek nearby and it wasn't too far to haul water in buckets. Chio was the cook in the vaquero camps, and in the days before the bunkhouses were built he'd keep big pots of stew cooking all day over an open fire. Chio was his nickname. That's what everybody called him. He was a hell of a nice young fellow and a very good camp cook. He came from San Juan Capistrano and he cooked in the vaquero camps on the Santa Margarita for years. He had a chuckwagon which was a kitchen and grocery store all in one. He didn't have the facilities to bake bread, so we always had tortillas when we were out in the vaquero camps. He'd take the dough and pat it between his palms until it was five or six inches wide and then put it on a grill over the fire. We thought his tortillas were great. And for meat Chio always had bacon, just like the bacon you buy in the store today. Charlie Hardy would send it up on the train from his packing house down in San Diego. If Chio ran out of bacon, some of the boys would drag a steer into camp and one of them would hit it on the head with the dull side of an ax and they'd butcher it. Chio would always use some of the meat to make beef jerky. There was lots of beef jerky in the vaquero camps. Chio would tie a rope between trees and cut the meat into strips about as wide as a piece of bacon and hang the strips on his line. He'd salt and pepper it and put other spices on it and leave it to dry in the sun. We'd keep a piece of jerky in our pockets to chew on during the day, and if we were going to be gone from the camp all day we'd put a tortilla and some jerky in our pockets and that would be lunch.

One of the characters in the vaquero camp was Tiano. Tiano was an old man and he always wore a straw hat. He took care of all the saddle horses for the vaqueros while they were in the camp. I notice in the movies now they refer to it as a 'remuda,' but we called it the 'campanera.' It was up to old Tiano to see to it that these horses were saddled and ready for the vaqueros when they woke up on the ground every morning. They didn't have a corral for these horses and they didn't tether them at night. So, the horses were just turned loose and they would feed in the creek beds or wherever there was grass. But horses are pretty constant in their habits and they usually stayed together at night, so they weren't too difficult to round up in the morning. And Tiano always kept a bell mare with the horses. That was an old mare who had ceased to be an active worker and had a cowbell around her neck. She was the one the other horses grouped around. Sometimes I'd wake up in my sleeping bag in the middle of the night and hear the clanging of her bell somewhere off in the darkness. One horse would be kept in camp, tied up during the night so that in the morning Tiano or his helper would have something to ride to get the campanera. When Tiano got older, he had a boy who helped him with his duties. And, in the morning, Tiano or this helper would mount this horse and follow the sound out to the bell mare and drive the campanera toward the camp. Then the men would go out with their tie ropes which were usually made of horsehair. They'd pick out their horses and tie the ropes around their necks and lead them over to saddle them. After the men had left camp, what was left of the campanera would be turned out to graze again. The vaqueros usually changed horses during the day, and Tiano had to have horses ready all day and take care of the tired ones, too. He cared for a string of forty or fifty horses. That was his responsibility.

It was also Tiano's job to see to the welfare of all these horses and he was very careful with them and expected the men to be, too. If a vaquero cinched a cinch too tight or left a crease in the saddle blanket, the horse would get an open sore on his back. Then Tiano would have to put this grease ointment on it, and he wouldn't allow anyone to ride that horse until the sore was healed. The horses were too valuable to be mistreated in any way. Any kind of cruelty to the horses was not tolerated. None of the men would be cruel to the horses, even if they got uncontrollably angry. All the riders wore spurs, but only for controlling the horses and not for punishing them. The rowel is the wheel at the back of the spur and the rowels on the Santa Margarita were pretty big, but they were not sharp. The horses were well trained, and if you wanted your horse to do something you'd just have to touch him with the rowel and he'd respond. There was no need to gouge the horse with a sharp rowel and if your spurs injured the horse in any way, Tiano would be sure to give you a sharp reprimand.

When John and I were riding with the vaqueros, Tiano always gave us the same horses. Mine was named 'Cuca' and John's was 'Paharo Blanca,' white bird. They were fairly old horses and they were probably given to us because they were well trained and because they were slow and tired, the kind of horses that even little boys like us could handle.

Tiano always wore a straw hat and he used to tell me this story every time I stayed in the vaquero camp. As I say, he was a very old man and he talked in a deep, gruff voice in broken English: 'Your grandfather was a very fine man. You know what he did for me? You see that?' And he'd show me his hand. It had no thumb. 'I was roping one day. . . .' You know they take the vuelta around the saddlehorn (to wrap the rope around the saddlehorn when roping a steer) and, if your thumb was accidentally caught in the rope when it tightened up, it would take your thumb off. '...and I lost my thumb one day. You know what your grandfather did for me? He sent me to a doctor, he gave me five dollars and this hat! He was a very fine man.' He thought that my grandfather was very generous.

Jome, if you ever write about this, one of the most important facets you should include is the relationship between employer and employee. It was a lot different in those days than it is today. Now it's pretty cold-blooded, but employees get more money and benefits. But, then, there's not that feeling of understood mutual respect. At least I don't think there is. I think that's been lost. The vaqueros worked all of their lives on the ranch. They considered themselves, and they were considered by my grandfather, and, later, by my uncle, to be part of the ranch. Steve Peters spent his whole life on the Santa Margarita and the relationship between him and my grandfather and my uncle and the children was a very personal one. Nobody would ever think of firing Steve Peters. It would be like tearing down the ranch house. Today, it seems funny that old Tiano would be grateful to my grandfather for five dollars and a new hat in compensation for the loss of his thumb. I don't think people today could understand it. That's how much things have changed.

On the Santa Margarita, they used two terms, rodeo and branding, and there was a distinction between them. The term, 'rodeo,' was used to refer to the rounding up of cattle when a cattle buyer came to the ranch to do business. A branding was just that. Brandings were usually held in the corrals because it was easier that way, whereas rodeos were often held on large, flat, treeless areas without ground squirrels. It was very dangerous to ride in an area with ground squirrels because the horses would stumble in the squirrel holes and both the horse and rider could be seriously injured. So, when they chose the site for a rodeo, the absence of ground squirrels was a primary consideration. But brandings ordinarily took place in corrals. They were held in the spring and early summer before the calves were weaned from the cows. The newborn calves didn't have brands, of course, and they would follow their mothers for some time after birth. Then you could tell that the calf should have the same brand as that of the mother. So they would round up all the mothers and calves in an area and drive them to the corrals. Then the calves would be separated from their mothers and dragged one by one

Steve Peters branding, as Carl Romer watches from the corral fence.

into the corral to be marked, branded and cut. These poor little calves would cry for their mothers and the vaqueros would rope them and pull them into the corral. There, a group of men would wrestle a calf to the ground and one man would hold a front leg with his knee across the calf's neck and a second man would hold down the hind quarters. The vaqueros would have a fire burning in one corner of the corral and they'd have a half dozen branding irons in it. One of the men would bring over a red-hot branding iron and press it on the calf's hind quarters. Smoke would come up from the calf's flank along with the smell of burning hide and hair and the calf would bawl with its eyes bulging out. I was a boy from a ranching family and I knew I wasn't suppose to, but I always felt sorry for the calves. Incidentally, the brand they used on the Santa Margarita was the TO brand. It was a T with an O at its base and my grandfather did not inherit the brand from the Picos or the Foresters. In the 1880's right after my grandfather bought the ranch, he went down to Texas to buy some cattle to restock the Santa Margarita herd and some of these cattle were branded with the TO. So, when he got them back to the ranch, he decided to adopt that for his ranch brand. There were no state brand laws in those days so nothing prevented him from adopting any brand he wanted. It wasn't until 1913 that California formed laws requiring that all brands be registered, and by that time the Santa Margarita had been using the TO for years.

After the calf had been branded, another man would come along with a sharp knife and he'd castrate this little calf if it was a male. The testicles of the male produce hormones that create muscles, and if these males were allowed to go uncastrated they would develop tough muscle as they grew and their meat would not be at all good for eating. Besides, ranchers improve their herds through selective breeding by buying certain bulls with the characteristics they want to breed into their herds. But the castrations are really pretty bloody affairs to watch. When they cut the testicles off, there is quite a bit of blood and the man doing the castrations usually wears some kind of apron and his hands and apron are covered in blood by the time the branding is over. The vaqueros called the testicles 'huevos' which means eggs. They would throw the huevos into the branding fire and let them sizzle for a while and take them out and eat them. This was supposed to be a delicacy and I ate them because every one else ate them, but I never liked them. This was all part of the very manly ritual of branding. Once in a while, some ladies would want to come and see the branding and Uncle Jerome would bring them down in a buggy or buckboard and the women would ask what it was that the men were eating. That was a very embarrassing question for Uncle Jerome to handle, because in those days matters of that nature were not discussed in front of ladies. Now, they are politely called 'Rocky Mountain oysters' and you can find them on restaurant menus in cattle towns all over California at the right time of year. But, back in those days, Uncle Jerome passed very lightly over the subject and the women politely didn't pursue it.

After the calves had been branded and castrated, they would paint tar over the wound to stop the bleeding. And, at the same time, a man notched the calves' ears with a knife. They always gave each calf an earmark to help identify it and this was done by cutting off a piece of ear in a certain pattern. And all the while the calf would bawl and his eyes bugged out and his tongue flapped around. Branding was hard work and necessary to the running of the ranch, but I never enjoyed it much.

Dad stopped talking for a moment, searching for what he wanted to say next. He looked annoyed at himself when it would not come to him and looked around as if some clue were on the floor or on the wall. When he glanced at the sidetable on his right, he saw the photo lying just where he'd put it and, relieved, he picked it up and continued:

Now this picture is unusual. It was taken at the San Onofre corrals in 1916. This group of people happens to be a movie company. This was in the early days of the movies and Uncle Jerome gave the movie company permission to use the ranch for some of their scenes. They used the cattle in the movie, so they were at the San Onofre corrals when this shot was taken. The movie company brought along their own still photographer who took this picture and they gave Uncle Jerome a copy. That's Carl Romer with the bowtie. And that's Uncle Jerome to the left of Carl. The woman is the female lead in the movie. Next to her is Mr. Hoskins, the cattle buyer from Hardy's packing house. The big man with his thumbs in his belt is the star, Roy Stewart. He was a great friend of the family's. Actually, he was one of Uncle Dick's drinking pals. Right next to Roy Stewart is Capitan, one of the vaqueros on the ranch. That's what makes this picture interesting: a movie cowboy standing next to a real vaquero. You can compare the two and see that the movie cowboy is romantic and colorful, but not very authentic.

130

The vaqueros didn't usually have a great deal of free time. If they were going to have a rodeo, then they'd work from sunup to sundown because the work had to be done. But then there might be a few days when there wasn't too much to do. The ranch was like a ship; there were always things to be done: check the windmills and the fences, check on a sick cow or repair equipment. The vaqueros took great pride in their personal equipment. They didn't make much money and they couldn't buy new equipment often, so they always repaired their own gear. If they had free time, you'd see them down at the bunkhouse or out in the vaquero camps working on their bridles or saddles or braiding their ropes. Particularly during the winter, when there wasn't as much work to do, they'd make their own horsehair ropes and some of them even made their own reatas. They had to supply their own riding equipment—saddles, bridles, all of it—and this equipment was their greatest pride. They had mail order catalogues for this type of equipment, and even though they didn't get paid much they'd spend what money they did have on top-of-the-line riding gear.

There were two saddleries they particularly liked: the Visalia Saddle Company of San Francisco, and Porter and Company in Arizona—Phoenix, I think. They'd keep the catalogues of these two companies around the bunkhouse and in them were pictures of saddles, spurs and bridles. These men liked to have the finest equipment. They might have started with an inferior saddle or at least not a very fine one and they'd keep and repair that one while saving for a topflight saddle. They'd pick their dream saddle out of one of the catalogues and save their money and, once in a while, look at the catalogue picture. Their equipment was uppermost in their minds.

There was no place for these men to go after work or on their days off because they were miles away from town. Once in a while, someone would get a wagon and take some of the men into town on a Sunday, but not very often. So they'd stay on the ranch for months at a time and there was no provision made for wives or girlfriends to visit. Even Steve Peters' wife and family never came to the Santa Margarita. They lived in San Luis Rey, and in the winter when there was not much work to be done, Steve would take a week off occasionally and visit his family. But there was no provision for female entertainment among the men. Naturally, I never thought about it at the time but, looking back on it, it's strange that these men would be happy under those conditions. Today, you'd have to go to town to raise hell once a week, but they didn't do that. The town was too far away.

There was never any trouble between the men—no slitting of throats or fist fights or any of that—none that I remember. There were plenty of firearms in the ranch house that had been collected over the years, but nobody ever wore a gun. There was never any need. Oh, I remember once someone brought a bottle of whiskey from town and gave it to the blacksmith at that time, a fellow named Joe, and he got drunk. While he was drunk, the whole operation shut down because there was nobody to fix the plows or any of the metal equipment. But we had very little serious trouble and I don't think the Santa Margarita was any different from other ranches around there in that respect.

So, the men didn't go anywhere when they had free time, and they had very few amusements of any kind. They played poker nearly every night. They didn't play for high stakes. It was more of a fun game and they'd let us kids play once in a while. I think they let us win occasionally and we'd all sit around the table in the bunkhouse or out at one of the vaquero camps with our cards held against our chests. Once in a while we'd peer carefully down at our hands.

These men all spoke Spanish, but I never did learn to speak it much. I knew some ranch Spanish about horses and cattle but I never learned much conversational Spanish, because the vaqueros always spoke to John and me in English. I think it was easier for them. They'd speak to us in English and to each other in Spanish. In the bunkhouse, they used barn lanterns for light, and while some of the men played poker others would read. Surprisingly, the men read a lot at night—mostly men's magazines and saddlery catalogues.

At night the family would sit up on the ranch house porch and off in the distance you could hear the vaqueros strumming their guitars and singing songs like *La Paloma* or *La Golodrina*. The men had no musical training, but they were twelve miles from town and this was their way of entertaining themselves. It was beautiful to hear.

At the ranch house Aunt Jane and Auntie Wee had a woman to do the laundry. It was her job to wash and iron at the ranch house. But the men down at the bunkhouse did their own laundry. The ranch provided brown soap and the men would take their dirty clothes down to the irrigation ditch that flowed past the bunkhouse. That's where they'd do their laundry. It was primitive, but they kept themselves pretty clean.

133

Once in a while someone would ask Uncle Jerome if it would be all right for an artist to come to the ranch to paint the local scenery. And the artist might stay at the ranch house for a day or two. On one occasion, two artists were staying at the ranch and painting at the same time. I think one was named Wendt, and another one had some Irish name like Kilpatrick. They were friends. They lived with the family at night and did their sketching during the day. And one day Mr. Wendt was out sketching and so was Kilpatrick. They were sketching in the same area but far apart. And Kilpatrick was having a hell of a time over a landscape with oaks and hills and cattle. And Wendt had finished his sketching for the day and was walking back to the ranch house. When he came up to where Kilpatrick was sketching, Kilpatrick said, 'Jesus, I can't get this damned picture right. It just isn't coming out for me.' Wendt said, 'Well, let me help you out.' So Wendt sat down and finished the picture. They both had painted this picture, which was quite unusual. So they brought the picture back to the ranch house. It was a typical California landscape. They didn't know what to do with it and they finally decided to give it to Uncle Jerome as a gift for letting them stay at the ranch. So this picture was signed by both of these artists and hung in the ranch house for years. I'd like to have it. It was a hell of a good picture, but when the ranch house things were being divided up, Uncle Dick got it. It's hanging in the board room of the Mission Viejo Ranch now.

There were many artists who came to the ranch to paint and this is the sequel to that story about Wendt and Kilpatrick: Father Mulligan was a priest from San Francisco who had gone to school with my uncles at St. Ignatius and was a close friend of the family's. Incidentally, he married my mother and father. He used to go down to the Santa Margarita to visit once in a while. I heard this story from him and I guess it's true. I hope a priest wouldn't lie. Anyway, I don't know if it was

Wendt or Kilpatrick, but this artist was at the ranch and he was interested in painting some of the local color that would be typical of the country. He met Steve Peters, who was, as I say, an impressive gentleman. He said, 'Steve, you've lived here all your life. If you were going to paint a picture, what would you paint?'

And, of course, Steve Peters was a completely uneducated person, but he spoke beautifully. He said, 'Well, Mr. Wendt, I'm not an artist like you, but I can tell you what picture I would paint.' He said he was born over in the San Luis Rey Valley which is the next valley over, south of the ranch. There was no real town there. There were a few little houses near the mission, little houses where Mexicans lived. He said, 'My family lived in a little house just down the road from the mission, maybe a quarter of a mile or so. We had a little yard in front of the house and a gate and the road to the mission went right by our gate. And we were very poor people and little boys like that in those days all wanted to be vaqueros. That was our ambition. There were several ranches around there, and when they were going to hold their rodeos all the vaqueros worked together, and they would gather just below our house in the early morning.' They would start before sunrise in order to get to the proper places to gather the cattle. This would be back in about 1860 or so, along in that era, long before my time, and things were still being done as they had been done for generations.

'The vaqueros would always gather below our house, maybe eight or ten of them, in the night. Just before dawn, they would ride up to the mission to get the blessing of the padre before they went out to do this dangerous work. When I was a small boy, maybe six or eight, I would go out to our gate and watch them ride up to the mission. They were all heroes to me. Dark, sun not up yet, and as they rode by, it was silent, except for the clump, clump, clump of the horses' hooves and the jingling of their spurs in the night, and nobody said anything. Then I'd follow them up to the mission and stand back of where they were. They would be in a semicircle around the door of the mission, and when the padre came out they'd get off their horses and fall to one knee with their reins over one shoulder, sombrero in one hand and the other hand up to their breasts, heads bowed. They'd stay still as statues, but the horses would be stamping their hooves and jangling their bits and it was so cold that I used to think that it was smoke coming out of the horses' mouths. Then the priest, in his Franciscan robes, would raise his hand for the blessing and the sun would just be coming up behind him. If I were an artist like you, Mr. Wendt, that's the picture I would paint.' But nobody ever did and I still think somebody could paint a magnificent picture, but it would take quite a good artist to do it.

CHAPTER TWELVE

Billy, Louie and Uncle Dick

SUNDAY MORNING *was the beginning of another beautiful day. My father slept later than usual, so Syd and I slipped quietly into the kitchen to make breakfast. We decided to eat in the sun and I set the table out on the patio. My father's eating habits were just that: strongly entrenched habits. The early riser in the family, he was used to cooking his own breakfast, and for as long as I can remember the menu was always the same: orange juice followed by waffles with lots of syrup and a pot of tea— oolong tea. He knew what he liked and saw no reason to experiment.*

He came in to join us just as the batter sizzled onto the waffle iron and the lid was closed. We had a few minutes to wait, drink our orange juice and talk. He took this opportunity to tell us what he'd discovered about the lighting in our dining and living room, the arrangement of the furniture and the orientation of the house itself. He wasn't judging; just observing the things that gave the room its mood and character. Breakfast was served on the sunny patio and it was a slow, leisurely meal—the way Sunday breakfast should be on such a fine morning. The conversation was light hearted, filled with good humor and sunshine and the smell of maple syrup. He mentioned Billy Magee in passing and Syd asked to know more about Billy. I switched on my tape recorder.

137

Aunt Jane had two younger brothers, Billy and Louie. They were the youngest of the Magees. Both of them worked for Aunt Jane for a while and Billy was hired by my grandfather to work for the Santa Margarita, too. Strange as it may seem, they went to college at Santa Clara. In those days there weren't any colleges that amounted to much in Southern California, so in order to go to college boys were very often shipped up north. Both Louie and Billy played football for Santa Clara. Louie was a quarterback and Billy was a fullback. Billy liked football so much that after he was finished at Santa Clara he played a couple of years for Stanford. They didn't have any rules in those days and he was a good fullback, so Stanford didn't mind. He was a great guy. There was never a dull moment with him around. Billy was just carefree, great big . . . he weighed 225 pounds . . . and he was entertaining. In those days we had to make our own amusements and people hung around Billy for a good laugh. Billy could always make you laugh. Uncle Dick and Billy always palled around together. When Uncle Jerome was gone for two or three days, Billy, Uncle Dick and Carl Romer would sit up at night and Billy would stand in front of the fireplace and tell jokes and recite Cicero in Latin. He had learned Latin at Santa Clara and he would stand in front of the fire with one elbow on the mantlepiece and recite the Cicero he had memorized in school, waving his arms and making these speeches in an overly dramatic voice. Everybody would cry with laughter. Billy was one of the main sources of entertainment on the ranch.

Carl Romer and Uncle Dick and Billy were always clowning around and playing practical jokes on one another. Up in the De Luz Canyon there lived a Mrs. Reagan and her daughter. They had a small house up there and Mr. Reagan was the owner of a big bakery in Milwaukee and wasn't often home. The daughter was a very pretty girl and Billy used to go up to see her. Once, Billy decided to bring a turkey and cook it for them, but at the last minute he got too busy and asked Carl and Uncle Dick if they could kill the turkey for him from the flock we had around the barnyard. For a joke, these two went out and shot a buzzard and put it in a bag and tied it onto Billy's saddle. He'd been working all day, so he didn't stop to examine it. When he got to the Reagan's, Billy proudly announced that he had brought a turkey for their dinner and held the bag by one end and shook the bird out onto the kitchen table. And out fell this dead buzzard. Both the women screamed in horror. Carl and Uncle Dick laughed about that for days.

Billy was always sneaking off at night and staying out 'til all hours. Carl Romer told me that there was an old barn up near Fallbrook. I don't know who owned it, but Billy and Carl would sneak saddle horses out of the ranch barn at night and ride up to meet a bunch of other fellows at this barn. They'd all put their horses in the barn and then go up to the hayloft and light a lantern. They'd sit around an old wire spool they used for a table and drink and smoke and play poker all night. Billy used to go up there quite often and get back just before dawn. Most of the time he didn't get even an hour's sleep because he had to get up before Uncle Jerome woke up. Everybody did. Billy was always on the borderline with Uncle Jerome. Uncle Jerome would always ask him questions for which he already knew the answers, just to see if he could trip Billy up. But Billy very rarely got caught. Even Billy Magee himself admitted to being the biggest liar the world had ever known. There was never a dull moment with Billy around.

Uncle Jerome did have a sense of humor, but at times it could be a little malicious. The Floods came down to the ranch to visit once a year or so. They would stay in their own private railroad car at one of the ranch sidings for a few days, maybe a week. Uncle Jerome would entertain them—have them up to the house for dinner or take them to one of the rodeos and that sort of thing. Once, young Jim Flood, the grandson of the Comstock Silver King, came down to the ranch with his father. He was about sixteen at the time and for some reason, he was accompanied by an older boy, a college student who went to Stanford and was acting as a companion for young Jim. Uncle Jerome had a real chip on his shoulder about college boys. He himself had only completed two or three years of high school at St. Ignacius before he was pulled out to accompany his father to the Chowchilla Ranch and he never went back to school. So he was a little suspicious of anyone with a college education and always anxious to prove that these college-educated people were not as smart as they were supposed to be. That's a funny thing, too, because it was Uncle Jerome who had encouraged and paid for the college education of both Louie and Billy Magee. He had financed their years at Santa Clara and he didn't seem to hold their college education against either of them. College was fine for them but for anyone else he just wasn't too sure.

But young Jim Flood brought this college boy down to the ranch with him one summer and you could see the hair on Uncle Jerome's neck stand up on end the very first time he met this boy. He was a very nice kid, about nineteen and had never been on a ranch in his life. But he was ready to try anything and I think Uncle Jerome was trying to trip him up during his whole stay at the ranch.

At dinner one night, Uncle Jerome looked up from his plate and peered down the table at this Stanford lad and said, 'Boy, you're in college so you're supposed to be pretty smart. Tell me, then, how do you

The Floods' private railroad car at a ranch siding.

square a circle? That's a little puzzle that a smart college boy like you should be able to figure out.' The boy thought about it for a moment and said he didn't know. But Uncle Jerome wouldn't let him off that easily and told him to think about it for a day or two. Then he abruptly changed the subject and announced that, after breakfast the next day, we were all going to ride over to a rodeo in the San Onofre Canyon, which was clear up at the other end of the ranch, a long ride. I don't think this Stanford boy had ever ridden a horse in his life, but he didn't say anything. He was Uncle Jerome's guest and Uncle Jerome said he was going to ride out to the San Onofre, so that's what he was going to do. I will say that Uncle Jerome made sure that he got a pretty tame horse that even a novice could handle and we all rode out to the San Onofre. The rodeo ended earlier than most, in mid-afternoon. Carl Romer had come out in the car and Uncle Jerome said that we could leave our horses with the vaqueros and ride back with him in the car. But he told the Stanford man that he wanted his horse back at the ranch house that night, so he would have to ride it back. And before the boy could reply, Uncle Jerome tapped Carl Romer on the shoulder and we were off.

It was a pretty mean thing to do to this kid. After spending all morning riding a horse, I'm sure he had painful saddle sores and it was a two- or three-hour ride back to the ranch house, if he didn't get lost trying to find it. We were all back at the ranch house for hours and the Stanford boy hadn't appeared. Finally, when it had been dark for an hour or so, Uncle Jerome sent Carl and me out in the car to look for him. We finally did find him. He had gotten lost and was just riding aimlessly around in the dark, cold, sore, tired and hungry. We put him in the car and I rode his horse back to the ranch house, which was easy for me to do. I had done it a thousand times, but I still didn't get to the ranch house until after midnight.

The next morning we were all pretty tired at the breakfast table but this Stanford boy was much more so because he wasn't used to this sort of life. And he sat down with the gentleness of someone who was not used to a long day in the saddle. My uncle was more cheerful than usual, bubbling with a good humor unusual for him. At the end of the meal, he

141

put down his coffee cup and smiled down the length of the table and said 'Well, boy, did you figure out how to square a circle?' The boy managed a polite smile and replied, 'No, sir, I can't figure that one out.' And my uncle said, 'It's really very easy. To square a circle you pound a square peg up a bull's ass.' And he laughed and laughed. I didn't want to but I laughed too and so did Carl. The Stanford boy tried a good-natured laugh but I thought he was going to cry. Carl and I were not laughing at him. We were laughing at the joke, but I don't think he knew that.

I always felt closer to Uncle Jerome's brother, Dick, because he had more time to spend with us kids and because you could always laugh with Uncle Dick. Uncle Dick learned to drive on the ranch and I liked to go with him because he was very kind to us kids. He had a white bulldog named Toro that was his constant companion. So, it would be Uncle Dick and Toro and me in the car while Dick was trying to get the knack of driving an automobile. The steering wheels of those old cars were made of wood and Uncle Dick would put a tack at a spot on the steering wheel so he'd know when the wheels were straight. But, then, he would watch that tack instead of where he was going and we would go careening around the fields. Dick would be so intent on lining that tack up with the radiator cap that he'd forget how to operate the brake. He'd shout, 'Whoa! Whoa!' as if it were a horse and then say to me, 'Jeromie, she's running away again.' And we'd just keep going until we got to a hill and then we'd stall going up the hill and stop. That was Uncle Dick's idea of driving a car. A few times he stopped the car by driving it into the river until we got stuck in the mud and then we'd have to walk through the mud back to the ranch house and get a vaquero to come down with a horse and pull us out. My mother didn't like my going driving with Uncle Dick, and looking back on it that's understandable, but he was her brother and she didn't want to disapprove of him to her children.

Even though Uncle Dick's driving ability was limited, he never did get into a serious wreck. He had more than his share of fender-benders, but he was never hurt and he never hurt anybody else. I remember one night Uncle Dick and Billy Magee were out together and I guess they were coming back to the Las Flores after a night of drinking in Oceanside, because just before they got to the Las Flores house, Uncle Dick skidded off the road and crashed his 1911 Franklin into a tree. Neither he nor Billy were hurt and the car wasn't too badly damaged either. But it had gone off the road and down an embankment where it hit the tree and they couldn't get it back onto the road. So Billy and Dick walked up the road in the dark until they got to the Las Flores and they took a dray horse and a lantern from the barn. Apparently, they weren't very quiet about it,

143

because the next morning Aunt Jane said that she had heard them laughing and talking all the way up in her room. They took this big horse back to the scene of the accident and tied a rope onto the bumper of the Franklin and got the horse to pull it up onto the road. But they were having such a good time that they overshot their goal and not only pulled the Franklin back up on the road, but all the way across the road and it rolled backwards down the other side of the bank and smashed the rear bumper into another tree. They both sat down in the lantern light by the side of the road and discussed what to do and finally decided to give it up for the night. So, they took the horse back to the Las Flores and went to bed. The next morning they found that the car was pretty beat up, but they were both fine except that Uncle Dick's gloves were smudged with oil. Uncle Dick was not what you'd call a careful driver, particularly when he and Billy were out for a romp.

He reached into his shirt pocket for a Lucky Strike and lit it with a match. He was looking through the haze of his own smoke for a long time with a laugh in his eyes, remembering Uncle Dick.

Chanquito Bailando. It means 'little dancing monkey.' I never knew his real name, but the men down at the bunkhouse named him 'Chanquito Bailando.' He was the herdsman for the milk cows, a little squatty man who'd carry the milk pails with his arms out from his sides with this bowlegged walk. So the vaqueros all called him little dancing monkey. His name was a joke around the place, but I don't think he minded it. He was a good-natured little guy. The reason I'm bringing him up is because of one of Uncle Dick's jokes. He couldn't resist a good prank. When I was about twelve years old, we all went over to mass at the San Luis Rey Mission. We didn't usually go all the way over there just for mass, but the automobile had come in by that time, so we went more often. The chapel at San Luis Rey was long and narrow, very much like the Santa Barbara Mission chapel and it had wooden pews. John and I were sitting in one pew and Uncle Dick and my brother, Richard, were in front of us and, in front of them, sat Chanquito Bailando and his

Uncle Dick, Toro, and admirer.

mother. Chanquito was all dressed up in his suit and he had a derby hat, obviously his pride and joy. His mother was more Indian than Mexican, a great big, heavy squaw sort of woman with a shawl over her shoulders. As you know, you stand up and sit down throughout a Catholic mass and when everybody was standing, Uncle Dick would lean over and slide Chanquito's derby right behind him so that when he sat down, he would crush his own hat. But Chanquito would turn and look every time and move the hat out of his way. You could hear Uncle Dick and Richard giggling and this went on all during the mass. John and I were giggling too, because we were just twelve and fourteen years old at the time. But here was Uncle Dick laughing and giggling during mass and he was well into his forties by this time. He never got Chanquito to sit on his hat, so at the very end of mass, he shoved it under his mother and she crushed

145

it flat. Uncle Dick and Richard were laughing so hard that they nearly fell out of the pew. Uncle Dick didn't intend to be cruel or mean and after the mass he met Chanquito and his mother outside of church and apologized and gave him ten dollars for a new hat. Uncle Dick wasn't as respectful in church as he might have been, but he had fun wherever he went, although it was kind of childish fun at times.

When my grandfather was alive Uncle Jerome was his aide, and among his other duties, he kept the books for the ranch. So, when my grandfather died and Jerome became the owner and manager of the whole ranch—the big boss—he hired a bookkeeper to keep the books straight and to act as a sort of general aide. There was a series of these bookkeepers. None of them stayed too long because it was not the sort of job that anyone would want for a career. One of the nicest book-keepers was a man named Ferris Kelly. He was in his late twenties and he worked for the ranch in 1917. I remember the date because the United States had just entered the First World War and everyone was very patriotic and very enthusiastic about the war effort. The war was upper-most in everybody's mind. I was fifteen at the time, so I was more excited about the war than most. Fort Kearny was a training camp down in San Diego where they trained soldiers before they went overseas. Sometimes, when Kelly and I were in Oceanside, we'd watch the troop trains pass through town and once in a while one of the soldiers would lean out the window and yell at Kelly, 'Hey, nothin' wrong with you. You're just a slacker.' Kelly wouldn't seem to hear it, but I always did.

Once, in the summer of 1917, Kelly and I and a bunch of the vaqueros went up into the Vallecito Mountains because there were reports of a mountain lion killing cattle up there. We didn't find any mountain lion or dead cattle, but when it was time to come home Kelly got a ride in one of the ranch cars and told me to take the horses back. I rode my horse and led Kelly's horse all the way back to the ranch house, but I was not happy about doing it. I can't remember why but I was angry at Kelly for leaving me to do this work. I was so mad that when I got back to the ranch house and had put the horses in the corral, I marched into Kelly's office and really told him off. It was wrong for me to do. I was about as temperamental and as hot-headed as any fifteen-year-old boy, but it was still wrong. And, to make matters worse, in the heat of my anger I called Kelly a 'slacker.' Today, a slacker would be the same as a draft-dodger, but the term was a very offensive slur in those days. At that time with all the patriotic feelings in the nation, to call a draft-age man such as Kelly a slacker was the gravest insult to a man's pride. Kelly was so upset at my outburst that he went to Uncle Jerome and complained bitterly about what I'd called him.

Later that afternoon, Uncle Jerome was sitting on the bench in the shade of the porch doing some figures in his notebook. I walked through the patio on my way to the kitchen when Uncle Jerome stopped me with the somber words, 'Jeromie, I want to see you over here, please.' I did not know what I had done, but I knew I was in some sort of trouble. Uncle Jerome lectured me for an hour, not loudly and angrily, but firmly and reasonably. He explained to me that calling Kelly a slacker was the worst insult I could have given. That a man's masculine pride was nothing for anybody to tamper with, let alone a fifteen-year-old boy. He explained that Kelly was an employee of the ranch and, as such, deserved the respect of everybody in the family and that I had acted like a spoiled little boy. He explained that what I had done was a terrible offense to Kelly, to the whole family and to all the other employees on the ranch. He wasn't angry or threatening but he was very stern and serious. I knew I was wrong and deserved being told so. Everything Uncle Jerome said was true. I think the fact that Uncle Jerome didn't yell at me made me feel worse. I'll never forget his lecture. I was so sorry that I would have cried right in front of my uncle if I hadn't been fifteen. Uncle Jerome ended by saying that Kelly deserved a sincere apology from me and that I should do it by the end of the day.

I went down to the barn to be alone and collect myself. When you're fifteen it's not easy to apologize, particularly when you are really sorry.

I was down in the barn thinking quite a while and I guess Uncle Jerome had been quietly keeping an eye on me, because he suddenly appeared in the doorway of the barn and warned me quietly, 'Jeromie, there's not much daylight left.' That's all he said and then he was gone. That's all he needed to say. There was no way out for me, so I just walked up to Kelly's office, still not sure what to say. I walked in and he looked up from his desk and I just began to stammer and then I started to cry. Kelly stood up and put his arm around me and said, 'Jeromie, it's all right. I know what you want to say and it's all right. Let's not talk about it any more. I'll tell you what I'd like to do. I'd like to walk with you down to the ranch house station and get the mail bag.'

That was one of the summers of the Texas fever tick and the ranch was divided into various sections by fences and all the gates were kept locked. For the rest of that summer I rode everywhere with Kelly, and when we stopped at a gate I'd get out and open it for him and then close and lock it after he passed through. That summer Ferris Kelly was my closest friend.

CHAPTER THIRTEEN

Conclusion

I HEATED MORE hot water for my father's teapot and he asked me what time his train was to leave. I told him, "Just after noon." He'd asked me the same question twice the day before. It wasn't that he was forgetful. The idea of missing the train always made him anxious, and during all his visits part of his mind was planning a last-day schedule so that he could get to the train with time to spare. It was an easy five-minute drive to the station, but he'd want to leave half an hour early. We didn't mind. If it gave him peace of mind, it was worth the wait at the train station. But the idea that his time was now limited to only an hour must have prompted him to finish his story, because suddenly he began:

The Santa Margarita, as I knew it as a child, does not exist any more. But the end of that era did not come suddenly. It was so gradual that I hardly noticed. Looking back on it, I can pinpoint those events that, for me, brought an end to this era.

Sing left the ranch for the last time when I was in high school. I guess by that time he must have been pushing seventy; I don't know how old he was. He was elderly anyway. He didn't look so ancient at that and he was still pretty active, but he had decided that enough was enough and he was going back to China. Apparently the Chinese of that period felt that they must go back to China to die. They didn't want to be buried in a foreign country. I can tell you exactly when this was. It was 1919 and I was sixteen years old. For a long time, my uncle's was the only car on the ranch. I guess they didn't feel they needed any more. But, by 1919, they had bought a couple of Model T's for the foreman to run around the ranch. They were Model T pickups with a bed in the back to haul hay and whatnot. My brother John and I were just learning to drive that summer and we were practicing by driving these Model T's on the ranch. This was in the summer of 1919 and it was the first time I ever drove a car and Sing was going back to China for good.

The day before he was to leave for China, he asked us if we would drive him to the Las Flores ranch house to say good-bye to one of his cousins who cooked for Aunt Jane there. I don't think they were actually relatives at all, but he called him cousin. He was younger than Sing. I can't remember his name—Hong or Ham or something. So, my brother John and I got the Model T and took him over to the Las Flores. We were very proud to be able to drive Sing to say good-bye to his cousin. Sing hadn't left the ranch house since his last visit to China, four years before. He never moved off the place, and so this was a big trip for him. When we got to the Las Flores, Aunt Jane was there, of course, and Sing went into the kitchen to talk to this cousin. They were in there for an hour or two, and I suppose Sing was going to say hello to this man's relatives in China and this was Sing's farewell trip so they were saying a long good-bye. But when they were finished they came out of the kitchen and we went to the car. When you left the Las Flores ranch house, you went out into the patio and instead of being surrounded by the house, the patio had a big, high hedge on one side. There was a gate in the hedge and that's the way you got to the car. So, we walked out of the house and across the patio and through the gate and Sing climbed into the car. John was driving so I sat in back. Sing's cousin stood with Aunt Jane on the steps. When we drove off, they could see the car for about a half a block before we turned around the barn and disappeared. The whole time, Sing looked straight ahead and his cousin looked straight at him. Nobody waved; nobody cried; nobody did anything. There was no display of emotion at all. It was an extraordinary thing because Sing would never see him again, but that was the Chinese way of doing it.

We drove him back to the ranch house and the next day he left. When he was about to leave the ranch house for the last time, everybody was very sad. It was a big deal. But Sing, himself, showed no emotion. He said good-bye and he wasn't very cheerful about it, but apparently crying or anything like that was not permitted. Sing had worked on the Santa Margarita for nearly fifty years, his entire adult life, and, to me, he was as much a part of the ranch as the ranch house itself. He had cooked and baked and collected his flour sacks and helped raise me and now he was leaving. Sometimes as a child, you're too young to understand what's

Sing's last trip to China, 1919.

151

happening. You're there but you just don't understand. For me, the day Sing left was the first time I can recall understanding what was going on and how I felt about it. I guess I was growing up, because I knew as much about how that day affected me then as I do now. Sing was a great man to me when I was a small child. He was very kind and good-natured and friendly and he cheerfully performed his cooking duties on the ranch for all those years. But it was a tragedy that this wonderful man had to work so hard and live his whole life separated from his own family just to support them. Of course I didn't realize it when I was very young, but Sing must have missed his family very much. But he never complained or even spoke of it. He was able to accept his life apart from his family and culture and cook all those meals for all those people for fifty years and still be so kind to us kids. Sing was a great man. After Sing left, nothing at the ranch seemed the same to me. His leaving was the first sign that a whole way of life was fading away.

Even before 1910, Uncle Jerome was the big boss. He oversaw every aspect of the running of that ranch. But after 1924 his health began to fail and another part of the Santa Margarita that I knew was fading out. In his last years, Uncle Jerome developed Parkinson's disease. He began to lose control of his nerves and he would shake. In our family, older people get Parkinson's disease. My father had it when he got older and I shake sometimes. It comes and goes, but sometimes my hand will shake so badly that I can't sign my name and for no apparent reason at all. My Uncle Jerome had the shakes and they got pretty serious. It was in his right arm and it would shake all the time and sometimes it would shake his head, too. Over the last few years of his life he began to deteriorate, and at the end he was taken up to San Vincent's Hospital in Los Angeles. He was up there about a week before he died.

He died of pneumonia about 11:00 at night and my mother was at his side. He had been slipping in and out of a coma for a day or two and everyone knew that it was only a matter of time. But just before he died, he came out of his coma and he looked at my mother with very clear eyes and asked to speak to Mr. Flood. My mother told him, 'Jerome, I think you had a dream. Mr. Flood is not here. He's up in his home in Lindenwood.' But Uncle Jerome told my mother that she was wrong and that Mr. Flood was there in the room with them. He said he wanted to talk with him about something very important. My mother explained that Flood wasn't there and tried to calm her brother down. Uncle Jerome sank back into the pillow and shut his eyes and died peacefully. Now, this Mr. Flood that I'm referring to was James Flood II, the son of the man who made the fortune in the Comstock. My grandfather and his father were the original partners who had bought the Santa Margarita. Uncle Jerome and James Flood II inherited ownership of the ranch from their fathers and were partners just as their fathers had been. A few minutes after my uncle died, a telephone call came in from Lindenwood reporting that James Flood II had died at 11:00 that night.

In those days, death was treated in a very formal way with every effort made to honor the deceased. Much more so than today. When my grandfather died in 1910, his body lay in an open coffin in the sittingroom of the ranch house. For a whole day and a night people came to pay their last respects before he was shipped up to San Francisco to be buried in the family plot in Holy Cross Cemetery. We children were paraded up to the coffin and a little step was put next to it so that we could kiss Grandpa good-bye. That was part of the ritual and I must admit not a very pleasant part for us kids, but we were expected to do our parts, and we did.

When Uncle Jerome died in 1926, John and I were going to college at Cal. My mother phoned us that Uncle Jerome had died in Los Angeles and that we should take the next train down to the ranch. It just so happened that the train we were on was the same train that also shipped Uncle Jerome's body to the ranch. So, when the train arrived at the ranch house station, we got off to find Steve Peters and a half a dozen vaqueros quietly waiting for the coffin to be unloaded. They were Uncle Jerome's pallbearers and they carried his coffin all the way up to the ranch house.

At the entrance to the ranch house was a bell that was rung three times a day to call the men to meals. It was also supposed to be rung in case of emergency, but in all the years I was on the ranch, I don't remember its being rung for anything but meals. However, when my grandfather lay in state in 1910 and in 1926 when Uncle Jerome's body was brought back to the ranch, the bell tolled continuously until the sun set. So, in 1926, when Steve Peters and the vaqueros carried Uncle Jerome's coffin up to the ranch house, the bell was ringing slowly and somberly and John and I followed this procession up to the ranch house.

His coffin lay in the sittingroom for the rest of the day and all that night. During the day, people came from Fallbrook and Oceanside and all the Magees came over from the Las Flores. They would come up to the coffin one at a time and kneel and say a short, silent prayer, walk over and talk in hushed tones to members of the family and then go home. This happened all day long, a continuous procession of people coming to say their good-byes to Uncle Jerome.

It was a part of this lying-in-state ritual that the body should never be left alone for its last night on the ranch. Some member of the family would sit in a chair beside the coffin and the family members would take turns at this throughout the night. The night Uncle Jerome was laid out in the sittingroom, my mother went into the kitchen where Steve Peters and Uncle Dick were talking and drinking coffee. Steve Peters spoke softly to my mother. 'Mrs. Baumgártner, I have stayed up with Mr. O'Neill a great many nights discussing business and, with your permission, I think I'd like to stay up with him tonight.' And he did. Steve sat with Uncle Jerome the rest of that night and in the morning Steve and the vaqueros carried the casket down to the ranch house station and put it on the train for San Francisco. As the train went through the ranch, people came down to the tracks to watch it go by as a way of paying their last respects. Once in a while there would be a vaquero on horseback in the brush alongside the tracks with his sombrero held to his chest, watching Uncle Jerome pass by for the last time. At the Las Flores, Aunt Jane and Auntie Wee and all the Magees were standing on the platform of Don Station when the train came through. People don't do things like that any more and it's too bad. That's the way it was done back then and it may seem pretty archaic and old-fashioned by modern standards, but it was a very nice way.

Whenever the family went into San Juan Capistrano, we'd always stop at Judge Egan's house. He was the only judge in the region, so he was the law for everybody and he was a good friend of my Uncle Jerome. I remember him as a very dignified man in a scruffy sort of way. He had white hair that was always longer than most people's, as if he'd forgotten to get a haircut. He had a white beard, a well-trimmed Vandyke that offset his unkempt hair and gave him an air of dignity. To me he looked like a character from *Huckleberry Finn*. He wore an old, rumpled, brown suit with a white shirt and a vest with a big gold watch chain across it with a mother-of-pearl watch fob hanging out of one vest pocket. He lived in a red brick house on the main street of San Juan Capistrano. It's still there, across the street from the old van der Leck house which is now a restaurant. Judge Egan's house was his office, too. That's where he held court. He was the telegraph operator for Capistrano, so he had his telegraph key in there, too. I guess the citizens of Capistrano were pretty law abiding because Judge Egan had the time to send telegraph messages as well as dispense justice. When we visited the Judge, we'd sit out on the wooden porch at the front of his house and the adults would talk and I'd sit there and listen to the telegraph key clicking in his office. Apparently he could carry on a conversation while keeping one ear on the clicking coming out the window, because sometimes he'd stop in mid-sentence and listen to the telegraph. Then he'd excuse himself and go inside and tap out a reply. When he was done, he'd come out and sit back down in his rocking chair and continue his sentence just where he'd left off. That used to amaze the adults and they'd always talk about it on the way back to the ranch. So, when I sat on Judge Egan's porch, I'd listen to the telegraph and to what Judge Egan

155

was saying so that I would know where he was in his sentence when he stopped. Then, when he started again, I would know if he'd lost his place in the sentence. I don't remember his ever losing his place. This was a little game I played while the adults talked.

Judge Egan was an old man when I was a boy and he used to shuffle his feet when he walked like he was sandpapering the floor. When the automobile became popular, he liked to sit on his porch and count the cars going by. The main highway ran through Capistrano in those days and on weekends many people would drive down to Tijuana and Judge Egan would count all the cars from his front porch and, whenever we'd visit, he'd always give us the previous weekend's car tally. Apparently he considered that one of his duties, too.

Occasionally, Judge Egan would come out to the ranch to visit or have dinner with the family, and when he did he always brought a bottle of whiskey as a present for my uncle. Uncle Jerome never drank, but Judge Egan would always give him a bottle of his whiskey as a token of thanks. Judge Egan used to buy whiskey by the barrel and I think he drank most of it himself, but he'd put some into a bottle when he wanted to give a gift. And it didn't have to be a whiskey bottle, either. Sometimes it'd be a ketchup bottle and the next time, a wine bottle. Uncle Jerome accepted these bottles from the judge and he stored them up in the attic. Over the years, many friends and business associates of my uncle gave him different kinds of liquor: scotch, bourbon, wine, champagne and all of it went up in the attic with Judge Egan's whiskey.

So, by the time Uncle Jerome died in 1926, there was a large collection of liquor up in the attic and it was all part of his personal property that had to be divided between the members of the family. I was between jobs at the time and so my family sent me down to collect our share of the liquor. This was right in the middle of Prohibition so everyone was more aware of the existence of this liquor than they might otherwise have been, and the equitable division of it was important for peaceful relations between the branches of the family. It's not that people didn't trust members of their own family, but this was Prohibition and that made this liquor a family heirloom of unique value. So, I was the emissary from our side who was supposed to oversee the Baumgartner interests. Uncle Dick did not come down from Los Angeles, but a man from his bank came down to represent him at these august proceedings. I drove down with my mother's chauffeur, Marshall, and we stopped along the way to collect cardboard boxes to put all the bottles in.

When all was ready, we all gathered in the dungeon. There was a trapdoor in the ceiling of the dungeon and we put a ladder up through it and crawled up to see what was up there. There was much more liquor there than any of us had imagined—hundreds of these bottles. So, it took us several days to get them down and put them into boxes. With all that liquor lying around, it was not surprising that at the end of the first day Billy Magee came by at dusk to say hello and have a drink with us. Among the other things Billy told us was the story of the old lady that lived in the attic and sneaked around at night, peering down through the vents. Then, later on, Auntie Wee assigned us all our sleeping rooms. She put me down in Uncle Jerome's old room and she put Marshall in the dungeon. As everybody was leaving the room to go to bed, Marshall grabbed my sleeve and said, 'Mr. Jeromie, I've got something to say for sure. I'm not sleeping in this room unless you take down that ladder and close that trapdoor. I'm not about to make it too easy for that old lady to come after me!' This was very serious to Marshall. After what Billy had said about the old lady's ghost, he couldn't sleep staring up at that open trap door. And every night after we'd finished packing liquor, Marshall would make us take down the ladder and close the trapdoor and I don't think he slept very well even then. But we were done in a few days and Marshall and I followed the truck back to San Francisco. Because it was Prohibition, we had to have a special permit to transport this liquor and we hired a trucking firm to handle it for us. On the way to San Francisco, we stopped at Uncle Dick's to drop off his share and then we drove home. I remember that we gave the truck driver a few bottles of whiskey to take home to his wife. When our family divided up their share, I got a lot of Judge Egan's whiskey and I still have some left. I trot out a bottle on special occasions and pour a sip for everybody, but only a sip and only for very special occasions.

In 1928, my parents went to Europe, and after they had left Aunt Alice became very ill. John and I were in college at the time and quite often we went to visit her. It was clear to us that she was dying. During one of our last visits, she whispered for me to bend down so that I could hear her better. She said, 'Jeromie, I have something I want you to have. I've been saving it for you. And I'd like to see Dick and your mother.' I told her that my mother and father were travelling in Europe and they wouldn't be back for some time. She said in that case she would like to see Dick anyway. She hadn't seen or spoken to her brothers and sister since my grandfather had died years before, and it was her dying wish to do so now. John and I phoned Uncle Dick down in Los Angeles and he took the next train. We picked him up at the station and drove him to the old house and took him upstairs to Aunt Alice's bedroom. In spite of all his monkeyshines, Uncle Dick was a very kind person and he was very emotional. He hadn't seen his sister in twenty years and he was very nervous as he climbed the stairs to her room. When both of those people looked at each other, they just broke down and cried. It was sadder than any scene in any movie, seeing those two old people cry after all those years. When I drove Uncle Dick back to the railroad station, he was still so upset that I didn't think he could make the trip back to Los Angeles. Aunt Alice died a few days later.

All families have problems and some of them they create themselves. Aunt Alice was close to her family and very close to us children. But just because of her loyalty to her husband, she wasn't able to speak to her brothers and sister until she was on her deathbed. Sometimes families get their values turned around. Some principle or insult becomes more important than a member of the family and in the end everybody regrets it. Uncle Dick was the only one who got to see his sister before she died.

Uncle Jerome had died a few years before without a word to her. My mother was in Europe. Aunt Alice died before she could give me whatever it was that she'd saved for me and I never found out what it was.

By 1941, the eldest of the Flood girls had married a New York banker. He was from the East and all he knew was stocks and bonds and banking, so he wanted to sell the Flood share in the Santa Margarita. It was decided that the families involved should settle accounts with each other by dividing the ranch. The Floods took the southern half, the half with the ranch house, and the Baumgartners got the San Onofre and San Mateo canyons up to the Orange County line. Uncle Dick took the part of the ranch in Orange County, the Mission Viejo and the Trabuco. I was working for the Mark Hopkins Hotel in San Francisco then. My brother Richard had died by this time, so in the Baumgartner family there was only John, Bessie and I. The three of us decided that John should come down from San Benito County and run our portion of the ranch and that I should investigate the possibility of building a luxury hotel on the beach at San Onofre. We were planning a resort like the Coronado in San Diego or the Biltmore up in Santa Barbara. By that time, John was an experienced rancher and he could manage that land better than anyone else. However, profits in the ranching business depend on a fluctuating market. So, a cattle ranch, even one expertly managed, can have a period when it is being run at a loss. If we built a hotel on the San Onofre beach, the money we made from the hotel would help offset any temporary losses in our cattle business and we'd have little danger of having to sell the ranch as so many other ranchers have had to do. As it turned out, the hotel idea would have worked and worked very well. Since the Second World War, both Los Angeles and San Diego have grown tremendously and the hotel would have been located halfway between the two and close enough to serve both. San Onofre beach is one of the finest beaches on the West Coast and a luxury hotel between Los Angeles and San Diego would have been a gold mine.

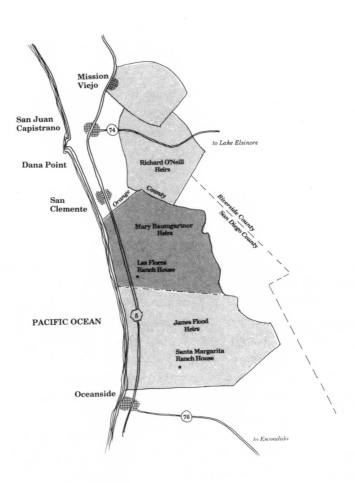

The Baumgartner part of the ranch was 55,000 acres with seven miles of beach front and John came down to manage it. We were going to call it 'Rancho San Onofre' and John even had a new brand made up for it. Not long after John had arrived, we got a phone call from one of the bookkeepers over at the ranch house. Two big military footlockers had arrived on the train from Oceanside that morning and the bookkeeper wanted to know if we knew anything about them. We decided that they must have been sent to the Navy base in San Diego and somehow put on the wrong train. But the next morning, a Major General Joseph Fegan arrived at the ranch house and announced that the government was taking possession of the ranch to use it as a Marine base for the duration of the war and that he was to be the commander of the new base. The Santa Margarita ceased to exist as a ranch at that moment. John had studied all his life to operate the Santa Margarita and almost as soon as he took it over, the government stepped in and made it Camp Pendleton. Nobody had forewarned us or discussed it with us. The government's idea of an announcement was the arrival of those two footlockers.

Naturally we were stunned, but at first under the Second War Powers Act, the Marines were entitled to use the ranch as a training base only for the duration of the war. We could see that was reasonable, considering the circumstances. But during the war, the Second War Powers Act was amended so that after the war the military could terminate its lease or take outright ownership of the ranch. When the war ended, John went to Washington and met with the Secretary of the Navy to plead for the return of the ranch to its rightful owners. But, by that time, the Marines had found Camp Pendleton such an ideal training base that they were determined to keep it. The Santa Margarita had every type of terrain that they wanted for training: beaches for amphibious landings, mountains, hills, canyons and even a tropical area in De Luz Canyon. So, the Marines paid the Floods and the Baumgartners four and a quarter million dollars and took everything south of the Orange County line.

The only part of the ranch that the Marines didn't take was Uncle Dick's part, the Mission Viejo. In 1941, when we divided the ranch, the

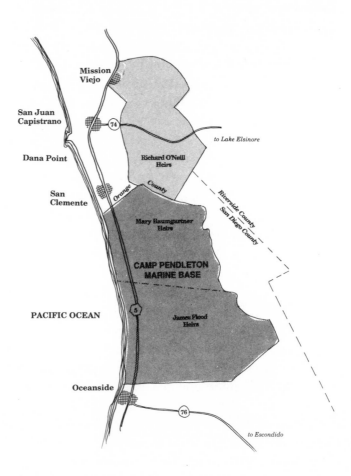

Floods wanted the southern part; John thought that the San Onofre was better suited to ranching than the Mission Viejo and Uncle Dick's family got the Mission Viejo because that part of the ranch was better suited to agriculture. Uncle Dick could lease out parcels of the Mission Viejo to farmers and the rents would provide a substantial income. Aunt Daisy was unhappy with this arrangement at the time because the O'Neills hadn't gotten any beachfront. Uncle Dick's children and grandchildren still own the Mission Viejo and they've done very well with it. They've sold off several thousand acres to a development company to build the town of Mission Viejo. Now, I read that they are developing the Trabuco Canyon area into a community like Mission Viejo. They're going to call it 'Rancho Santa Margarita' after the original ranch. I suppose they want to keep the Santa Margarita name alive, but their part of the ranch was never part of the original Santa Margarita grant. As I understand it, this new development is to be a planned community for 50,000 people. So, they've done very well with their part of the old ranch. The Marines never made adequate use of the San Onofre coastline and finally gave it to the State of California for a park.

After the war and after the ranch was lost, John went back up to San Benito County and began ranching again. He had the TO brand registered and that part of the Santa Margarita Ranch is still active in the cattle business and carries on the family heritage. He has become one of the most honored ranchers in the state. But I sometimes wonder what would have happened to us if we still ranched the San Onofre and had built that hotel.

The history of the Santa Margarita is closely associated with the book, *Ramona*. It was written by Helen Hunt Jackson who was a writer of the time and a do-gooder, I guess. She had a reputation in the East as an author of some merit. She came out west to write about the plight of the Indians. She wanted to write a novel that would draw the attention of the American people to the sad condition of the Indians of California. So, she wrote the story of Ramona, which became a bestseller of its day, and it's still a good story of early pastoral life in California. She came out to do some research and visited the ranches around the Santa Margarita to get local color for her novel. She stayed on the Santa Margarita for a while and then at the Guajoma with the Couts family. But she got into some kind of a battle with Cave Couts and my grandfather when they found out that she was siding with the Indians in her story and was putting the ranchers in a bad light. So, she packed up and moved to the Camulos Ranch in the San Fernando Valley and finished her book there. But a lot of the characters and locations that she used she'd gotten from her stay in the Santa Margarita area. and she wove her story around the characters she had met there.

If you read *Ramona,* the main story evolves around a part-Indian girl who was the adopted daughter of one of the old California families. This girl fell in love with an Indian and wanted to marry him, but of course her family didn't want their daughter marrying an Indian. She married him anyway, supposedly at what they call Ramona's Marriage House in San Diego. Incidentally, that was Aunt Jane's family home before the Magees moved up to Fallbrook. The people on the Santa Margarita claim that Helen Hunt Jackson got the idea for her story from the life of the Couts girl. In the time before my grandfather came to the Santa Margarita, when the Forsters still owned the ranch, one of the Couts' girls over on the Guajoma Ranch wanted to marry an Indian boy and ran away from home to stay with the Forsters. Steve Peters, later the head vaquero of the Santa Margarita, was a young man at that time and he took this girl from the Guajoma Ranch, helped her across the river and brought her to the Santa Margarita. Helen Hunt Jackson was supposed to have taken that incident and based her Ramona story on it, but there actually never was any Ramona. She was a fictional character. But the book was very popular, sort of a cross between *Gone With the Wind* and *Uncle Tom's Cabin.* Everybody read it.

After the war, your mother and I took you and your sister down to the ranch. I particularly wanted Auntie Wee to met you kids. Aunt Jane was dead by that time and Auntie Wee was the last of that generation of women who had raised me. She still lived in that little house by the beach in Oceanside and we visited her one afternoon. You were probably too young to remember this. We went down to the beach, and while you and Mary played in the water, Auntie Wee and your mother and I sat up on the sand talking. We talked about many things and she was telling us about her girlhood. When I was a child on the ranch, I didn't know that Auntie Wee was half Indian. It was never discussed. But as I grew older and found out, I began to think about Auntie Wee and this Ramona story. Auntie Wee was half Indian and she was raised in what they later called Ramona's Marriage House and she had never married. So, that day on the beach I said, 'Auntie Wee, tell us about Ramona.' When Auntie Wee talked, she used her hands in a beautiful way to illustrate what she was saying. It was a characteristic of that generation of Spanish people. She used her hands in this graceful way and while we were talking to her she was running sand through her fingers. But when I asked her about Ramona, she stopped moving her hands and looked me right in the eye for a long time, thinking. Then she looked down at her hands and picking up a handful of sand, watched it run through her fingers and said proudly, 'Jeromie, Ramona still lives. I can't tell you any more, but Ramona still lives.' And that's all she would say on the subject. Auntie Wee always thought that she was Ramona. And maybe she was.

The youngest of the Magee family was Louie. He was Aunt Jane's youngest brother and he was the last manager of the Las Flores. He married Ruth Wolfskill and managed that part of the ranch for years. When the Marines took the ranch in 1942, the government gave Louie and Ruth special permission to live at the Las Flores for the rest of their lives. In 1962, when I was down in San Diego, I phoned Louie and he invited me to come up and stay the night at the Las Flores. He was awfully glad to see me and we sat down and had a couple of bourbons and talked. He did most of the talking. He wasn't too clear about contemporary things but he remembered well. He said, 'Jeromie, there's nobody left around here to talk to anymore because everybody's dead.' So, we talked all night and I learned a lot that either I hadn't known or had forgotten.

Besides being very religious, the Magees were all very superstitious. To them, miracles were likely to happen and ghosts might appear at any time. Such things were never far from their minds. So, of course, the Las Flores ranch house was supposed to be haunted. Aunt Jane had a sister named Antonia. Everybody called her Toni and she'd come to visit her sister and usually stayed overnight and when she did, Toni and Aunt Jane would sleep together in the big Victorian bed up in Aunt Jane's bedroom. This bed had a great big headboard and a rail that ran straight across the foot of it. In the middle of the night they were awakened by someone mumbling and they sat up in bed and saw two Franciscan monks standing at the foot of the bed saying their rosary. Toni and Aunt Jane grabbed each other and the priests said, 'Be calm, my children,' and they turned and walked out of the bedroom. These were not girls; by this time they were grown women. When Billy and Louie finally calmed them down and they told their story, they both had seen the same thing. They told about these monks in their gray robes. Well, Louie had been to Santa Clara by that time and he was pretty well educated. He asked them if they didn't mean brown robes and the women said that the priests were wearing gray robes. Louie had learned up at Santa Clara that the earliest Franciscans in California wore gray robes and that Franciscans took to wearing the brown robes long before these women were born. Neither women knew that Franciscan priests ever wore gray robes, but they said that was what they saw. So, all the Magees were sure that these were the ghosts of priests who had lived at the Las Flores in the Spanish days when there was a little assistance mission there.

There's a humorous footnote to this story: They used to tell it in front of us children and it scared the hell out of us. I think that is why we always slept with Aunt Jane, because we were afraid to sleep alone. I was probably only about four or five when I first heard this story and I misunderstood it. When they said that they woke up and saw these two monks at the foot of the bed saying the rosary, I thought they meant monkeys! For years I thought they had seen two monkeys sitting at the end of the bed praying. I didn't find out that they meant priests until I grew up, but after that, the idea of monkeys at the foot of the bed was still more frightening than priests to me. So, I guess I was more scared by the ghost story than any of the other children. That night that Louie and I stayed up so late, I asked him about that story and he said, 'The robes were gray and not brown, so I guess that proves they saw ghosts.' Until the day he died he would tell you the story was true, and Louie was no dummy. The Magees were like that.

We got up the next morning about 7:30, I suppose, and over breakfast started kicking around the old times and the old stories again. I told Louie a story about his brother, Billy, that he'd never heard: Once he was out at the San Mateo house at Christmas time. Rodriguez lived there with his wife and children. They had all kinds of kids, from little babies to teenagers. Billy could speak Spanish very well because it was part of his life. So, he was talking to these children and doing little magic tricks for them and found out they had never heard of Santa Claus. He told them all about Santa Claus and then said, 'Santa Claus is going to come this year.' He didn't have any equipment to dress up like Santa Claus, so he found a pair of red long johns. He went out to the stable and collected as much horse hair as he needed. He found an old pair of deer antlers hanging up in the barn and went out behind this little hill at the back of the house. He got into his red underwear and glued the horsehair on his face and tied the antlers to an old burro they had back there. He had someone say that Santa Claus was coming and here came Billy with these horsehair whiskers and a sack over his shoulder, leading this damn burro with the deer antlers tied to its ears. He said he had a hell of a nice Christmas and the kids all thought Santa Claus was great. Louie hadn't heard that story and I think he was glad I told him.

Louie and I were still reminiscing about all these things when Ruth suddenly appeared and said, 'It's lunch time.' We'd been talking all morning and we hadn't even gotten up from the breakfast table. So, we had lunch and I drove off. That was the last time I saw him. He died two years later in 1964. He was the last of the Magee family and the last of the people from my era to live on the Santa Margarita. They're all gone now.

He said this last sadly but very matter-of-factly. He took only a moment to reflect and then he was on his feet, heading to the bedroom to change for his train trip. It took little time before he was dressed in his suit and tie, suitcase in hand. We knew he would be anxious to go, so we left as soon as he was ready.

At the station, the passengers were already gathering, sitting on their luggage in the sunshine by the tracks, a little boy walking heel to toe on one rail. People were craning their necks to see the train way down the track. The train pulled in and we found his car without much trouble. Most weekenders were going home on coachcars, but my father always liked his own roomette. At lunch in the dining car, he would enjoy meeting and talking with the other passengers. But then he liked to retreat to the privacy of his own roomette. It was to such a place that he went when his eyes glazed over and he stroked his hair: a private little room to gaze off into the distance and remember.

The conductor took his bag and put it up into the vestibule. Syd kissed Dad on the cheek and he thanked her for making his weekend so pleasant. He turned to me and I broke custom by putting my arms around him and hugging him. He returned my hug warmly and gratefully. He stepped up into the train and disappeared. We stood back and waved at the dark tinted windows, not knowing which, if any, concealed his return wave. A knock on the train window to our right brought our attention to my father's face pressed up against the smoked window glass. We followed that window with our eyes and smiles and waves until the last car of the train disappeared around a distant curve.

BIBLIOGRAPHY

Interviews: Jerome O. Baumgartner—October 19-22, 1974, and February 14-15, 1975. Carl Romer—November 16-17, 1974. Inez Grant—November 30, 1974.

Brackett, R.W.: *History of the Ranchos of San Diego County.* San Diego: Federal Writers' Project; 1939.

Beck, Warren A., and Ynez D. Haase: *Historical Atlas of California.* Norman: University of Oklahoma Press; 1977.

Clay, John: *My Life on the Range.* New York: Antiquarian Press, Ltd.; 1961.

Cleland, Robert G.: *Cattle on a Thousand Hills.* San Marino: The Huntington Library; 1951.

Copley, James S.: *Historic Ranchos of San Diego.* San Diego: Union-Tribune Company; 1969.

Engelhardt, Zephyrin: *San Luis Rey Mission.* San Francisco: The James H. Barry Company; 1921.

Glasscock, C.B.: *The Big Bonanza.* Portland, Ore.: Binforts & Mort; 1931.

Gudde, Erwin G.: *California Name Places.* Berkeley: University of California Press; 1949.

Latta, Frank F.: *The Saga of Rancho El Tejon.* Santa Cruz: Bear State Books; 1976.

Lewis, Oscar: *The Silver Kings.* New York: Alfred A. Knopf; 1947.

Stephenson, Shirley E.: *John J. Baumgartner, Jr.* The Oral History Program, California State University, Fullerton; 1982.

Stephenson, Terry E.: *Forster vs. Pico.* Santa Ana: Fine Arts Press; 1936.

Stone, Irving: *Men to Match My Mountains.* New York: Doubleday & Company, Inc.; 1956.

Watts, Peter: *Dictionary of the Old West.* New York: Alfred A. Knopf; 1977.

Witty, Robert M., and Neil Morgan: *Marines of the Margarita.* San Diego: Frye & Smith, Ltd.; 1970.

The Oceanside Blade-Tribune: Nov. 19, 1898; Nov. 26, 1898; Dec. 1, 1900; May 17, 1906; June 26, 1907.
The San Diego Union: Feb. 17, 1881; May 17, 1884; May 8, 1910.
The Los Angeles Times: Dec. 11, 1949; Jan. 13, 1974.

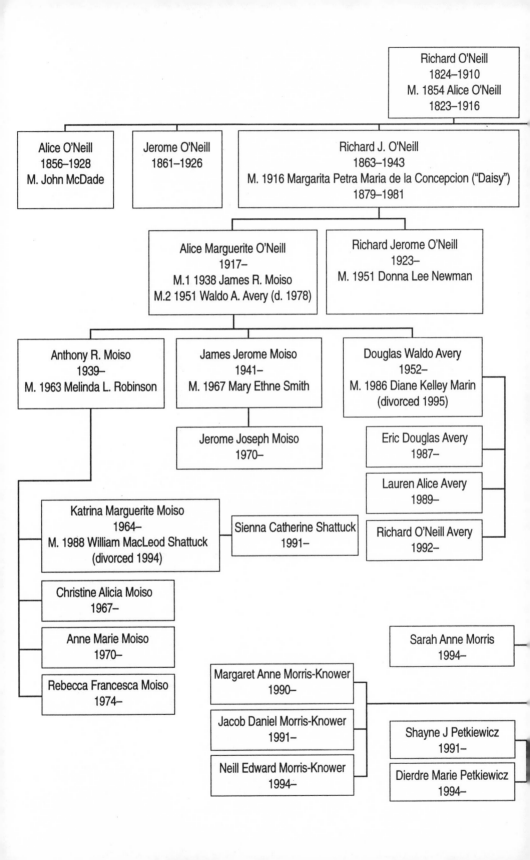

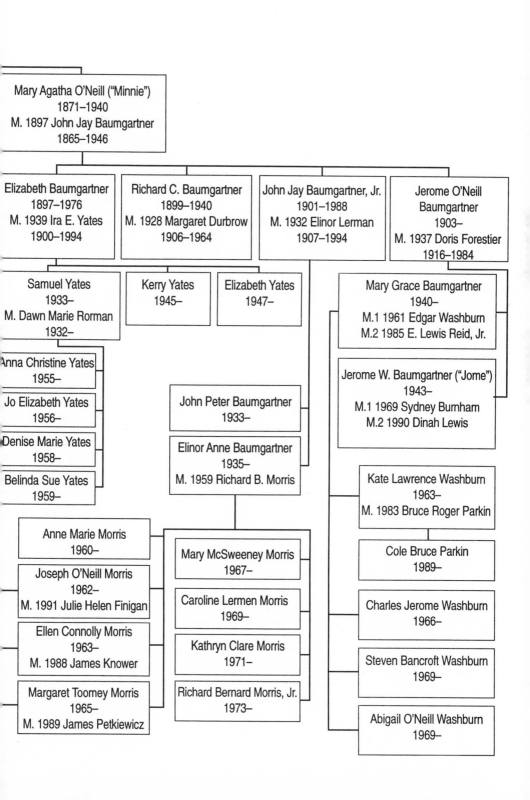